New Age Religion and Globalization

RENNER Studies on New Religions

RENNER Studies on New Religions is an initiative supported by the Danish Research Council for the Humanities. The series was established to publish books on new religions and alternative spiritual movements from a wide range of perspectives. It includes works of original theory, empirical research, and edited collections that address current topics, but will generally focus on the situation in Europe.

The books appeal to an international readership of scholars, students, and professionals in the study of religion, theology, the arts, and the social sciences. And it is hoped that this series will provide a proper context for scientific exchange between these often competing disciplines.

NEW AGE RELIGION AND GLOBALIZATION

Edited by Mikael Rothstein

AARHUS UNIVERSITY PRESS

Copyright: Aarhus University Press, 2001
Printed in Denmark by Narayana Press, Gylling
ISBN 87 7288 792 3

AARHUS UNIVERSITY PRESS
Langelandsgade 177
8200 Aarhus N
Denmark
Fax (+ 45) 8942 5380

73 Lime Walk
Headington, Oxford OX3 7AD
United Kingdom
Fax (+ 44) 1865 750 079

Box 511
Oakville, Conn. 06779
USA
Fax (+ 1) 860 945 9468

www.unipress.dk

Preface

In 1992 Danish scholars formed a network focusing on the study of new religious movements. This project known as RENNER (Research Network on New Religions) was based on a substantial grant from the Danish Research Council for the Humanities and proved to be a success. RENNER was in many ways able to further the academic study of new religions in Denmark, and this led to closer contacts with scholars abroad.

Following the original RENNER project, a new grant from the Research Council in 1998 allowed the work to continue in a more specific direction (under the name RENNER II) with an emphasis on new religions and globalization.

The scope of the globalization programme is, on the one hand, to expand our understanding of Western new religions in the international and intercultural context, but, on the other hand, to analyse the phenomenon of globalization itself through the study of globalized cultures such as most new religions. This is, of course, no easy task. During the past decades the scientific study of globalization has expanded rapidly, and many discussions pertaining to religion have emerged — including volumes dedicated to the investigation of new religions in globalizing environments — not only among sociologists of religions but also within the field of the history of religions.[1] This, however, is not the place to sum up the results and perspectives of scholarly discussions of globalization. This has been done brilliantly elsewhere, and the reader is referred to the selections of books and articles mentioned in the references (Beyer 1994, Robertson and Garrett 1991, Hexham and Poewe 1997, see also the references in the following articles). Considering RENNER's current project, though, a few remarks should be made.

---

1. In 1995, for instance, the International Association for the History of Religions (IAHR) dedicated a session to the subject at its XVIIth congress in Mexico City.

In the history of religions there are several instances of internationalization with a direct bearing on religion. The cultural processes of the Hellenistic-Roman Age are an example of many different cultures coming into close contact, leading subsequently to new kinds of religious communities and new religious beliefs and discourses. Similar developments are typical in the modern situation which allows detailed comparisons between past and present conditions, even with an emphasis on globalization (Warburg 1999). One thing in particular reveals itself as important in this connection: The historical perspective. Globalization is often understood to be a rather recent sociological development, but cultural processes of the past may owe more to the current situation than first imagined. Indeed, as pointed out by Frank J. Lechner, globalization is often rooted in long-term historical processes (Lechner 1998, 209). This was one of several reasons why RENNER held a conference in 1997 on the comparative study of new religions in the Hellenistic-Roman age and today's world (the proceedings were subsequently published in Bilde and Rothstein 1999), and the more specific interest in globalization partly emerged from the results of that initiative. In that sense RENNER's current aim is an extension of previous scientific perspectives. At the same time the globalization project takes the study of new religions into a field which has become increasingly more relevant to the study of contemporary religion altogether, thus placing the study of new religions in the only sensible context: in the history of the world's religions.

At this point, bearing the historical perspective in mind but focusing on globalization, two different ways of perceiving new religions or new kinds of religious consciousness emerge: (1) the study of globalized new religious organizations, and (2) the study of globalized new religious discourses or ideas — two perspectives that may well correlate, but sometimes do not.

Globalized new religious organizations may be defined as transsocietal religious cultures that, even when adapted to local conditions, basically remain the same where they appear (Rothstein 1996). Examples are in abundance: Most new religions are mobile religious cultures which simultaneously import into many different societies the same social structures and the same cosmologies. Groups such as Transcendental Meditation (TM), the Raelian religion, ISKCON, The Family Federation for World Peace and Unification (formerly the

Unification Church), The Family, and many others, may well adapt to local conditions, but at the same time they form a network of more or less identical communities around the world. To use historian of religions William E. Paden's term, such groups constitute different transnational and transsocietal 'Religious Worlds' in the sense that they 'create and occupy their own universes' independent of geographical position and societal context (Paden 1994, 51). Paden does not talk of globalized religions specifically, but the concept 'Religious Worlds' applies perfectly to what is seen in globally scattered new religious movements in terms of cross-cultural identification with fellow members living in other parts of the world. Globalized new religious discourses or ideas, however, are not defined by sociological structures in the same narrow sense, but may be seen as kinds of global cultures that — quoting anthropologist Ulf Hannerz — are 'carried as collective structures of meaning by networks' that are transnational and transsocietal (in Featherstone 1990, 239). Sometimes coherent belief systems are distributed through such networks. At other times single religious representations find their way around the world in the same manner.

The modern internationalization of New Age beliefs reveals how a religious discourse or belief system (however versatile) has become globalized even though no organization or no formal representation is at work. To a certain extent the spread of spiritualism in the 18th century is a parallel example of how a certain religious theme caught on in many different parts of the world in a very short time although no concrete religious body was carrying it. While globalizing religious organizations are easily recognized — not least because they usually find it important to identify themselves — it is much more difficult to specify the results of people who self-consciously cultivate 'an intellectual and aesthetic stance of openness toward divergent cultural experiences' (Featherstone 1990, 239). In both cases we encounter what Hexham and Poewe term the 'global dynamics of religious cultures' (Hexham and Poewe 1997, 40), but the kinds of dynamics are quite different.

RENNER has put an emphasis on both perspectives. The first conference of the globalization project addressed the latter by discussing the issue of New Age religion — a viable, non-institutionalized example of modern folk religion — and globalization. The conference,

which RENNER co-hosted with the Department of History of Religions, University of Copenhagen, took place in Copenhagen, Denmark, in November 1999, with participants from Denmark, England,
Holland, Italy, Norway, Sweden and the United States. All presentations were discussed among the contributors and a small number of
other interested scholars. These discussions allowed everyone to edit
their presentations according to the suggestions and comments made
by other participants. The articles in the present volume are the final
result of that process. The volume is divided into two separate sec-
tions, one dealing with general perspectives and another presenting
different case studies.

A subsequent RENNER conference will be devoted to the study of
a much less visible, but still globalized religious organization, the
Baha'i religion (to be held in August 2001). Finally, the issue of new
religions and globalization in general will be addressed at yet another international conference to be held in Denmark in 2002.

It is the hope of RENNER's board that new interesting results will
emerge from these initiatives, and that further discussions will bene-
fit from what will be presented in this and following publications.

I take this opportunity to thank the contributors for their obliging
and swift cooperation. Further I would like to thank the Danish Research Council for the Humanities for making the publication of this
book possible.

Mikael Rothstein
August 2001, Albertslund

Bibliography

Beyer, Peter 1994. *Religion and Globalisation*. London: Sage.
Bilde, Per and Mikael Rothstein (eds.) 1999. *Nye religioner i helle-
    nistisk-romersk tid og i dag*. Aarhus: Aarhus University Press.
Featherstone, Mike (ed.) 1990. *Global Culture*. London: Sage.
Hexham, Irving and Karla Poewe 1997. *New Religions as Global
    Cultures*. Colorado: Westview Press.
Lechner, Frank J. 1998. 'Globalization'. In: William H. Swatos (ed.),
    Encyclopedia of Religion and Society. London: Altamira Press, 208-9.

Paden, William E. 1994 (1988). *Religious Worlds. The Comparative Study of Religion*, Second edition. Boston: Beacon Press.

Robertson, Roland and William R. Garrett (eds.) 1991. *Religion and Global Order*. New York: Paragon House.

Rothstein, Mikael 1996. 'Patterns of Diffusion and Religious Globalization'. *TEMENOS*, Vol. 32, 195-220.

Warburg, Margit 1999. 'New Age og gamle dage. Religion og globalisering i dag og i hellenistisk-romersk tid'. In: Per Bilde and Mikael Rothstein (eds.), *Nye religioner i hellenistisk-romersk tid og i dag*. Aarhus: Aarhus University Press, 39-52.

Contents

Part I:

General Perspectives

Prospects for the Globalization of New Age: Spiritual Imperialism Versus Cultural Diversity

Wouter J. Hanegraaff

In order to get into the mood for writing this article, I typed in the word 'globalization' on my Internet search machine. To my considerable surprise, upon opening the very first website that appeared on my screen I found myself looking at the face of my countryman Ruud Lubbers,[1] the Dutch prime minister in the period 1982 to 1994. Having retired from politics, Lubbers now appears to be involved in issues of globalization, particularly from an economic perspective. As political leader of the Dutch Christian Democratic Party (CDA), Lubbers had been responsible for introducing a new style of 'no nonsense' politics based upon market economics. In so doing, however, he paved the way for the present reign of neo-liberal capitalism in the Netherlands which is represented by a political coalition that no longer includes his own Christian Democratic Party and has pushed the ideology of the market to a level that even Lubbers himself believes might have potentially dangerous moral and social implications. On his 'globalization' homepage, Lubbers primarily defends the values of democracy and market economy, but also calls attention to issues of spirituality. His statement remains quite vague. In any case, his own Roman-Catholic roots are clearly apparent and his idea of 'spirituality' is certainly very different from a New Age perspective.

Ruud Lubbers' ideas of spirituality may indeed be of little interest

1. www.globalize.org

in themselves, but I did perceive a symbolic significance in the fact of meeting this politician and economist as a primary representative of 'globalization', since it squarely places issues of spirituality in the economic context of a global market based upon the values of democracy. In very general terms the claim I wish to make is that the globalization of New Age spirituality is more appropriately seen as an aspect of global Americanization. American values of democracy and religious freedom are intimately linked to the New Age phenomenon of a 'spiritual supermarket', where customers pick and choose the spiritual commodities they fancy. But while this market system is based upon the recognition of individuality and diversity, its basic rules are themselves not subject to negotiaton by any of its customers: the global market system as such is essentially imposed upon individuals and cultures, whether they like it or not. They are free to choose within the limits of the system, but hardly have a chance to choose whether they want that system in the first place. Clearly it would be a sentimental misconception to perceive the global market as an example of the various cultures of the world 'growing closer to one another'. Rather, out of hard economic necessity they are forced to participate in a global system, and free choice is possible only within the limitations and according to the basic rules of that system. In short: one is allowed free choice *within* the system, but one cannot choose another one.

Solving the Problem

This constellation is essentially similar to New Age visions of the globalization of spirituality. Since the origins of the New Age movement in the 1950s and 1960s and throughout its development and consolidation during the 1970s and 1980s[2] and up to this day, countless authors have repeated the same message: we need to 'heal the world', put an end to global fragmentation by a new vision of planetary wholeness, and bring the cultures and religions of the world together by overcoming dogmatic boundaries and emphasizing the universal wisdom traditions common to all of them.[3]

2. On the phases of development of New Age religion, see Wouter J. Hanegraaff, 2001.
3. See, e.g., Hanegraaff 1996, 330-61.

That one certainly does not need to be a New Ager to share such sentiments is demonstrated by the many popular songs on this theme. If well-orchestrated and produced — preferably with a children's choir and burning candles — songs like Abba's 'I have a Dream' or Michael Jackson's 'Heal the World' are a recipe for success. At the very moment I was writing these lines, the radio in the background was playing yet another example of such a song, this one emphasizing that 'we've got to live together',[4] and I found it significant to hear the longing for unity expressed, among other things, as the need for humanity to 'find the answer' and 'solve the problem'. This formulation touched a string, for it sounded precisely like popular New Age visions about the way towards world harmony. This vision consists of a few easy and logical steps:

— There is a 'problem': worldwide fragmentation, in the form of wars, religious strife, and so on.
— This problem obviously needs to be solved, and the way to do so is to change our consciousness.
— Once this transformation of consciousness has occurred, the problem will obviously have vanished. Enter the New Age of Light and Abundance.[5]

4. Lisa Stansfield, 'Live Together' (L. Stansfield/I. Devaney/A. Morris).
5. Among countless examples, see the relatively sophisticated example of the physicist David Bohm. Bohm's influential *Wholeness and the Implicate Order* begins by identifying the problem: 'fragmentation is now very widespread, not only throughout society, but also in the individual; and this is leading to a kind of general confusion of the mind, which creates an endless series of problems and interferes with our clarity of perception so seriously as to prevent us from being able to solve most of them' (p. 1). Bohm continues by stating that this situation can only be remedied by changing our 'general forms of thinking' (p. 3): '... what should be said is that wholeness is what is real, and that fragmentation is the response of this whole to man's action, guided by illusory perception, which is shaped by fragmentary thought. ... So what is needed is for man to give attention to his habit of fragmentary thought, to be aware of it, and thus bring it to an end. Man's approach to reality may then be whole, and so the response will be whole' (p. 7). Even Bohm's style of writing reflects the influence of the Indian thinker Jiddu Krishnamurti on his ideas. (See Hanegraaff 1995).

The logic of the argument is straightforward enough, and the underlying sentiments are certainly understandable and commendable.
But what has struck me again and again is the almost complete lack
of interest among its representatives for the obvious practical and
theoretical objections to it, as well as the casualness with which an
obviously culture-specific, American approach is believed to be a
blessing for cultures based upon entirely different foundations. As
for critical objections: these are dismissed out of hand as a reflection
of 'negative thinking' — which is the very thing that prevents 'solving the problem' in the first place.[6] 'Positive thinking', in contrast,
seems to imply that critical questions should be ignored wherever
they threaten to rear their ugly heads.[7]

I will ignore the most obvious of these objections, i.e. the question
of *how* this global transformation of consciousness is supposed to be
brought about. New Agers have several answers, in terms of inescap-
able cosmic laws of spiritual evolution, the attainment of a 'critical
mass' of enlightened consciousness, an intervention by the Forces of
Light, or a combination of these.[8] More difficult, more frequently
ignored, but also more interesting, is the question of what the new
global spirituality is supposed to look like in practice, once it has
arrived. For here we encounter the fundamental paradox of a spiritual vision that proclaims the supreme holistic value of 'unity in
diversity'.

Unity in Diversity?

New Age visions of a global spirituality and a united world are be-
devilled by a fundamental contradiction that seems to be integral to
the very core of their worldview. On the one hand, fragmentation is
wrong and wholeness is good; therefore we need to have an over-
arching global spirituality transcending the doctrinal boundaries that
separate the religions of the world. But this very rejection of the religious dogmatism and exclusivism of established religions is based, on

6. See, e.g., Hanegraaff 2001, 330-61.
7. Sanaya Roman 1986, 63: 'If you hear people speaking of negative things
    immediately send them positive pictures and change the conversation'.
8. Hanegraaff 2001, 344-56.

the other hand, upon a strong emphasis on the values of religious freedom and individuality. Clearly, it follows that the ideal of a universal global spirituality should not infringe on the right of individuals to choose the religion they want.[9] The problem is obvious. As long as individuals will be so kind as to select the right type of universal spirituality — that is to say, as long as they share the essential spiritual beliefs of the New Agers themselves — they are free to be as diverse as they please in all other respects. But what if they use their individual right to religious freedom to choose an exclusivist and dogmatic religion that rejects the very idea of a global spirituality as misguided and wrong, perhaps even evil and satanic? Won't such dissidents from the vision of global spirituality be seen as misusing their freedom? And if so, how will the representatives of a global spirituality respond? Try to convert the dissenters? Or simply impose the 'right' spirituality on them? Let us imagine, for a moment, that the New Age had actually eventuated and that new global spirituality had become the norm; would exclusivist dissidents be sanctioned as heretics and forced into the mould?[10]

Some New Agers are bound to respond that such critical questions merely demonstrate that the critic is still sadly locked in limiting thought-patterns that belong to the past. In the New Age, people's consciousness will have changed so that they will simply turn away from 'limiting', exclusivist and dogmatic forms of religion and towards a holistic spirituality. This will happen by itself, as a result of the natural evolution of consciousness. But if so — the critic is bound to continue — what will be left of the cherished values of free choice and of diversity? Will people be free only to make the right choices, not the wrong ones? Would not all forms of spirituality start to look more and more alike? Would there be any room left for creativity? Or would any initiative of spiritual innovation be smothered immediately, resulting in an essentially static and conservative religion that would no longer evolve or change? What would be left of the cherished principle of spiritual evolution? Would human history have come to an end? Wouldn't the world begin to look suspiciously like the very thing that the New Age doctrine of reincarnation was

9. Ibid., 340.
10. Ibid., 329-30.

supposed to supplant: an essentially static heaven of harmony and bliss, but also of boredom — a heaven on earth in which nothing new and interesting can be expected to happen for the rest of eternity?

The Monistic Pathos

As far as I am aware, New Agers almost without exception ignore such questions. Confronting them means questioning the basic principle of holism: a principle which does not amount to a doctrine or belief system but is an example of what the historian of ideas Arthur Lovejoy refers to as the 'monistic pathos'. I quote:

> That it should afford so many people a peculiar satisfaction to say that All is One is, as William James once remarked, a rather puzzling thing. What is there more beautiful or more venerable about the numeral one than about any other number? But psychologically the force of the monistic pathos is in some degree intelligible when one considers the nature of the implicit responses which talk about oneness produces ... again, when a monistic philosophy declares, or suggests, that one is oneself a part of the universal Oneness, a whole complex of obscure emotional responses is released.[11]

Such talk of 'obscure emotional responses' is not intended in a depreciating way: as Lovejoy rightly indicates, precisely such responses are of supreme importance to understanding the history of ideas in the first place, and obscure does not necessarily mean irrational or ridiculous.[12] My point is merely that holistic visions are based not on reason but on emotions. There is nothing wrong with this, but the fact needs to be recognized. The question imposes itself how the emotionally-motivated dream of an emerging global spirituality relates to the realities of the so-called globalization of New Age.

11. Arthur O. Lovejoy 1964, 13.
12. See the brilliant article by Thomas Bredsdorff, 1975, 1-27; cf. Wouter J. Hanegraaff, 1995, 99-129, especially 113-17.

A Research Agenda

The 1992 volume *Perspectives on the New Age*, edited by James R. Lewis and J. Gordon Melton, contains several case studies of the acculturation of New Age in non-western contexts. Rosalind Hackett, Mark R. Mullins and Gerhardus C. Oosthuizen discussed the cases of Nigeria, Japan, and South Africa respectively.[13] I think that approximately nine years after these studies, it would be important to initiate a special research program focusing on a much wider range of countries; and such a research project should be steered by some general systematic questions and principles. I would like to mention four of them.

1. Research should be based upon clear definitions of what we mean by 'New Age'. In the articles I just mentioned, the term is used quite loosely as including almost anything of an 'alternative' western-esoteric or occultist nature, or even as a near synonym for 'New Religious Movements' as such. For example, Hackett discusses movements such as AMORC, the Aetherius Society, the Swedenborgian Church, Eckankar, Subud, Baha'i, Soka Gakkai, Nichiren Shoshu, Hare Krishna, the Unification Church, and so on.[14] In my view, this means that she is not actually speaking about the globalization of New Age, but simply about the spread and missionary activities of various New Religious Movements beyond their countries of origin. These phenomena are fascinating to study, but do not necessarily have anything to do with the New Age movement.
2. The question should be faced: to what extent is it possible, even theoretically, to conceive of the existence of a 'New Age movement' in non-western societies? According to my own condensed definition, New Age is 'characterized by a popular western culture criticism expressed in terms of a secularized esotericism'.[15] New Age is characterized less by what it asserts

13. Rosalind I.J. Hackett, Mark R. Mullins, and Gerhardus C. Oosthuizen, in Lewis and Melton 1992.
14. Hackett, 1992.
15. Hanegraaff 2001, 520-21.

than by what it rejects: all forms of New Age are united in their rejection of dualism and materialist-reductionism, and this culture criticism is expressed in terms of heavily secularized interpretations of western esotericism.[16] If my definition of New Age is accepted, the obvious question arises: how to conceive of a movement based upon popular western culture criticism in a non-western society. Can such a movement only be transplanted from the west without much chance of taking root in a non-western culture? And if it does take root there, for what reasons could it possibly be expected to have popular appeal?

There might be an interesting paradox here: if New Age is defined in terms of its reaction against basic aspects of dominant western culture, especially its dualist and materialist-reductionist heritage, then one would expect New Age movements in non-western countries to criticize the very phenomenon of a cultural imperialism that attempts to impose these western (and especially American) values on indigenous cultures. Accordingly, one would expect New Age movements to exalt the local spiritual traditions of the countries in question and try to present them as compatible with New Age worldviews, so as to oppose the combination against the dualist and reductionist worldviews of the west. Actually, however, the case studies I mentioned convey the distinct impression that the trends referred to as 'New Age' may pay lip-service to local spiritualities, but actually function as missionary movements spreading an essentially western esoteric message to non-western countries, with very little concern for the local traditions of those countries. In other words, they themselves seem to be aspects of a western spiritual imperialism instead of a counterforce against it: the leading idea is that New Age beliefs should be accepted by non-western cultures. This phenomenon of an implicit New Age ethnocentrism is actually not surprising at all. It strongly confirms my analysis of New Age religion as a paradoxical phenomenon that is profoundly influenced by the very same culture it criticizes. Against this background, it is hardly surprising that in 1993 the Lakota Indians published an official declar-

---

16. Ibid. For these aspects, see 515-17, and 411-513 respectively.

ation of war against the New Age movement, accusing its representatives precisely of ethnocentric arrogance and disrespect for
their sacred spiritual traditions.[17] Similar reactions are to expected
in non-western countries and continents other than the United
States and Western Europe.

3. This brings me to my third point: academic research of the acculturation of New Age in non-western societies should not focus
merely on documenting the presence of western esoteric groups
and initiatives in non-western countries. It should explore the
more interesting question of whether, and if so, how New Age
movements in these societies interact with local spiritualities, and
especially whether New Age spirituality takes on new forms in
the context of non-western cultures. I suspect that this does not actually happen to any deep extent, and that the attempt to impose
a spiritual 'unity' based upon American values and presuppos-
itions usually takes precedence over the laudable ideal of honouring 'diversity' and allowing native traditions to influence and
transform American-style New Age perspectives. This suspicion
is based on what I have read about the spread of New Age beyond
Europe and America, but more research would be needed to see
whether it is correct. If my suspicion would be borne out by further investigation, it would confirm my thesis that the globalization of New Age is essentially a form of spiritual imperialism.

In this context, it is interesting to take notice of a passing remark
by Rosalind Hackett in her research on Nigeria. She found that
'African spirituality has not been viewed as a source of wisdom,
nor commodified or appropriated by the New Age in the same
way as Native American and Australian Aboriginal teachings'.[18] I
suspect that this may be a reflection of the social segregation
between blacks and whites in American culture. It is well known
that American New Age spirituality is essentially a white phenomenon. Upper- or middle class American whites may have a

---

17. *Evangelische Zentralstelle für Weltanschauungsfragen* 57, 7 (1994). Cf. Armin
Geertz 1996, 395: 'Native Americans play a decisive role as symbols in
New Age ideas and rhetoric, but Native Americans themselves play a
role only in as much as they conform to New Age market stereotypes'.
18. Hackett 1992, 217.

romantic fascination for the oppressed spiritual traditions of native Americans or Australian Aboriginals, but this fascination
does not include African traditions, which tend to be associated
with the 'otherness' of black Afro-American culture at home. In-
grained stereotypical associations between black Africa and
'primitive magic', as opposed to an elevated spirituality focusing
on light and love, are yet another obvious example of the West-
ern/Christian heritage of New Age spirituality.[19] Even if such politically incorrect ideas are not openly expressed in New Age literature, they are implicitly present in the very type of spirituality that
it presents. For example, whereas the well-known New Age ico-
nology of Jesus and other Ascended Masters is evidently based
upon models such as Warner Sallman's famous 'Head of Christ'
and its countless copies,[20] it is practically impossible to imagine a
negroid — or even a distinctly Jewish! — Christ as symbolizing
New Age ideals[21]. This is just one more indication that New Age
ideals of 'unity that honours diversity' actually imply a unity
based on white anglo-saxon puritan (WASP) models, that will
prove oppressive of real spiritual diversity.

19. One is surprised to find such stereotypes even in the writings of vocal de-
fenders of 'magic'. The influential New Age neopagan Stewart Farrar described three waves of emigration from the submerged continent Atlantis. The first one, dominated by what Farrar calls the 'Power Ray', crossed
northern Europe and Asia; it was a 'contaminated and dangerous stream'
characterized by cults of 'primitive power magic'. Farrar (1983, 26-27)
contrasts it with a second emigration wave dominated by the 'Wisdom
Ray' and culminating in 'the great mind-mastering philosophies of the
East', and a third one dominated by the 'Love Ray' and flourishing in 'the
Egyptian, Tyrian, Greek, Hebrew, Christian and Moslem achievements'.
Black Africa as such is not even considered worthy of mention in Farrar's
narrative, but the general line of argument clearly reflects stereotypical
oppositions of 'primitive magic' against the 'spiritual East' and western
scriptural religions as the most highly-developed form of spiritual consciousness. To find such ideas in a defense of modern witchcraft is as
bizarre as it is revealing about the implicit ethnocentrism at work in New
Age perspectives.
20. See David Morgan, 1998.
21. See, e.g., Fred Carter (1987), reproduced in Morgan, 1998, 38.

4. Finally, there is a fourth point I would like to make. Particularly in the case of phenomena such as esotericism and the occult, ethnocentrism is a temptation not only for New Agers but for researchers as well. In his article on New Age in Japan, Mark R. Mullins claims that

> the founders of many Japanese new religions have functioned essentially as traditional shamans and articulated the basic worldview of traditional folk religion. ... these movements are most accurately understood as a new expression of folk religion and a revival of animism. The 'new' syntheses of both indigenous and foreign beliefs and practices in various movements over the past century have not fundamentally altered the cosmology and framework of traditional folk religion.[22]

On the face of it, Mullins seems to be saying that — in Japan at least — New Age religion does allow itself to be transformed by local traditions rather than just trying to impose an alien religious system on them; and he might also be construed as confirming, in a way, the idea that New Age spirituality is essentially not a culture-specific but a universal phenomenon, so that it is easily accommodated by local manifestations of it. But actually I am afraid that his interpretation is a mistake, resulting from the impact of western ethnocentric theories about religion combined with an essentially non-historical approach. Concepts such as 'animism' or 'magic', and closely related concepts such as 'the occult', 'the primitive' or 'superstition' have been construed by western scholarship as universal and essentially static phenomena of human culture;[23] and as such they have been opposed to the specific, unique and dynamic historical phenomena of their own culture: Judeo-Christian religion, and progress by means of rationality and science. I suggest that this view is fundamentally flawed: phenom-

---

22. Mullins 1992, 242.
23. See, e.g., Bronislaw Malinowski 1992, 70 (essentially repeating J.G. Frazer's perspective), on the monotony of magic: 'Follow one rite, study one spell, grasp the principles of magical belief, art and sociology in one case, and ... adding a variant here and there, you will be able to settle as a magical practitioner in any part of the world ...'; and cf. Hanagraaff forthcoming 2002.

ena such as magic and the occult are quite as dynamic and subject to historical change and cultural variation as any other type of religion.[24] The so-called 'animistic' or 'magical' traditions of Japanese religion are necessarily different from similar traditions in western esotericism, and new combinations of Japanese shamanism and New Age shamanism should be recognized as yet another new and historically innovative phenomenon. I do not buy the idea that all these phenomena are 'essentially' or 'fundamentally' the same, merely because they are being thrown into a theoretical wastebasket referred to by names such as 'animism' or 'the occult'.[25]

In sum: systematic research into the globalization of New Age spirituality should take into account at least four things. Firstly: it must be based upon clear working definitions of New Age. Secondly, if New Age is a movement of western culture criticism that is nevertheless deeply influenced by the very culture that it rejects, researchers should be extremely sensitive to the complex dynamics of ethnocentrism (and particularly krypto-ethnocentrism) in processes of New Age acculturation. Thirdly, and closely connected to my second point: attention should be focused on the extent to which New Age spirituality takes on new forms under the influence of specific non-western cultural contexts, and systematic comparisons should be made in this respect between processes in different countries and on different continents. Fourthly, researchers should be wary of how ethnocentric theories of 'magic', 'the occult', 'animism' etc. can blind them to processes of historical change, so that phenomena of innovation and diversity are tacitly sacrificed to a misleading theoretical unity that exists in the mind of the scholar rather than in the realities he is studying.

In Defense of Relativism

I would like to close with addressing an issue that cannot be avoided in any critical discussion of globalization: the supposed danger of relativism. Salman Rushdie recently caused consternation again, this

---

24. Hanegraaff 2001, 406-10, especially 407.
25. See detailed discussion in Hanegraaff 1998, 253-75.

time due to an open letter to the sixth billionth citizen of the earth;[26] United Nations secretary-general Kofi Annan withdrew his preface to the book in which Rushdie's letter was to be published, because he could not endorse Rushdie's militantly anti-religious humanistic message. What shocked me in Rushdie's letter was not his dogmatic anti-religiosity (to me, that aspect was simply another example of a somewhat old-fashioned type of secular humanism rather closely linked to Rushdie's generation and likely to lose ground and credibility as time goes on). I was far more concerned with the anti-relativist implications of his message. Taking as his example the case of the circumcision of women, Rushdie rejects what he calls the 'brain-dead' idea that the Universal Declaration of Human Rights is culture-relative, thus allowing these types of practices to be accepted as the expression of a specific culture.

While I share Rushdie's horror of these particular practices, I do belong to his category of 'brain-dead' relativists, and make no excuse for it. From what I have said previously, the reader will have gathered that I am not only sceptical about the idea of a globalization of spirituality, which I consider ill-founded and impossible to realize, but that I also consider this idea to be dangerous. The ideals — like Rushdie's humanitarian ideals — are understandable enough, and the underlying motivations are quite commendable, but the call for unity cannot but lead to totalitarianism; world unity according to western models will take the form of imperialism; and the belief in a global unity that honours diversity is a pious dream incompatible with the basic ideal itself.

Such conclusions might possibly be dismissed as a statement of personal belief on the part of this particular scholar, but that is an interpretation I would contest. Rather, I claim that they are a necessary implication of historical and anthropological research. What we *know* is that people, cultures, and spiritualities are different. Taking this fact of diversity as given, one may certainly wish to explore the question of what unites them in spite of differences. In itself such an exploration is quite legitimate, and it may help to break down unnecessary barriers between people and cultures. But the conclusion that

26. http://www.tribute.nl/wpf/uk/content/speciaal.html#book

the similarities between religions discovered by such research should then be allowed to overrule the differences, only leads to bad scholarship as far as academic research is concerned, and results in oppression when it comes to politics. Now, the claim for an emerging global spirituality is essentially political in nature, and my suggestion is that scholars should not lend themselves to giving credence to it.

The 'spectre of relativism' is actually not a spectre at all.[27] From a scholarly perspective — that is to say, one that begins and ends with respecting the evidence — relativity in human culture is not a theory but a fact. Relati*vism*, in contrast, is a philosophical theory about the fact of relativity. This theory cannot be proved in a conclusive way, but neither can any of its rivals. My suggestion is that relativism should be given preference pragmatically, as a working theory, because it does not have any dangers comparable to the dangers of alternative theories, including Salman Rushdie's theory of secular humanism that includes the dogma of the universality of human rights. Obviously the Universal Declaration of Human Rights is a human invention: we know precisely who invented it and when. To what extent it will — or should — be accepted by non-western cultures is not a scholarly or intellectual question but a political one, which will (and should) be fought out not in scholarly circles but in the global arena of ideological and religious competition. In order to defend its tenets and fight against inhuman practices, one simply does not need these principles to be sanctioned by some kind of metaphysical authority, or by scholars who wrongly claim such authority. In fact, the attempt to obscure or deny the human and culture-specific nature and origin of such principles is a covert attempt to claim suprahuman and universal authority for one's own ideals; and such attempts are reflections of the will to power. That the ideals may indeed be highly commendable and worth fighting for is not the issue. The issue is that they still remain ideals, not objectively-established truths.

The same argument goes, *mutatis mutandis,* for New Age ideas of a universal spirituality. The empirical fact is that human cultural and religious values are relative. The New Age theory of a perennial phi-

27. Cf. Clifford Geertz 1984, 262-78.

losophy, which implies that such relativity is deceptive, may or may not be true; but it is and remains a metaphysical theory that can neither be proven nor disproven by reason or scholarship. The theory of relativism is a metaphysical theory as well, but one that may be preferred on a pragmatic level, as a working theory in dealing with the hard social and political realities of global diversity. The reason for preferring it is that it forces us to accept other cultures and religions as having the same rights to be taken just as seriously as we ourselves wish to be taken, and because it stimulates us to critically question the cultural biases that make us resist such an idea. No real discussion is possible without precisely these minimum conditions: listening to others, and being willing to question one's own pet ideas. New Age spirituality rejects relativism and fails to answer these minimum conditions (as everybody knows, who has tried to have a critical discussion with a convinced New Ager). As a result, in its attempts to 'heal the world', New Age spirituality cannot but fall back on the only alternative available: subtle or less subtle versions of the very religious authoritarianism and spiritual arrogance that it claims to supplant.

Bibliography

Bohm, David 1980. *Wholeness and the Implicate Order*. London and Boston: Routledge & Kegan Paul.

Bredsdorff, Thomas 1975. 'Lovejovianism — or the Ideological Mechanism: An Enquiry into the Principles of the History of Ideas according to Arthur O. Lovejoy' *Orbis Litterarum* 30.

Carter, F. 1987. 'Jesus Praying in the Garden'. Reproduced in David Morgan, *Visual Piety: A History and Theory of Popular Religious Images*,(1998). Berkeley, Calif.: University of California Press.

Farrar, Stewart 1983. *What Witches Do: A Modern Coven Revealed* (rev. ed., Custer). Washington: Phoenix Publishing.

Geertz, Armin 1996. 'Contemporary Problems in the Study of Native North American Religions with Special Reference to the Hopis'. *The American Indian Quarterly* 20.

Geertz, Clifford 1984. 'Distinguished Lecture: Anti Anti-Relativism'. *American Anthropologist* 86.

Hackett, Rosalind I.J. 1992. 'New Age Trends in Nigeria: Ancestral and/or Alien Religion?'. In: James R. Lewis and J. Gordon Melton (eds.), *Perspectives on the New Age*. Albany, N.Y.: State University of New York Press.

Hanegraaff, Wouter, J. 1995. 'Krishnamurti en "het einde van de tijd": De gesprekken met David Bohm'. In: Hans van der Kroft (ed.), *Waarheid zonder weg: 100 jaar Krishnamurti*. The Hague: Mirananda.

Hanegraaff, Wouter J. 1995. 'Empirical Method in the Study of Esotericism'. In: *Method & Theory in the Study of Religion 7, 2*.

Hanegraaff, Wouter J. 1998. *New Age Religion: Esotericism in the Mirror of Secular Thought*. Albany, N.Y.: State University of New York Press.

Hanegraaff, Wouter J. 1998. 'The Emergence of the Academic Science of Magic: The Occult Philosophy in Tylor and Frazer'. In: Arie L. Molendijk and Peter Pels (eds.), *Religion in the Making: The Emergence of the Sciences of Religion*. Leiden: Brill.

Hanegraaff, Wouter J. 2001. 'New Age Religion'. In: Paul Fletcher, Hiroko Kawanami, David Smith and Linda Woodhead (eds.), *Religion in the Modern World*. London: Routledge.

Hanegraaff, Wouter J. 2002. 'The Study of Western Esotericism: New Approaches to Christian and Secular Culture'. In: Peter Antes, Armin W. Geertz and Randi Warne (eds.), *New Approaches to the Study of Religion*. Berlin & New York: De Gruyter (forthcoming 2002).

Lovejoy, Arthur O. 1964. *The Great Chain of Being: A Study of the History of an Idea*. Cambridge, Mass.: Harvard University Press.

Malinowski, Bronislaw 1948. 'Magic, Science and Religion.' In: *Magic, Science and Religion and other Essays*. Glencoe: Greenwood Press reprint.

Morgan, David 1998. *Visual Piety: A History and Theory of Popular Religious Images*. Berkeley, Calif.: University of California Press.

Mullins, Mark R. 1992. 'Japan's New Age and Neo-New Religions: Sociological Interpretations'. In: James R. Lewis and J. Gordon Melton (eds.), *Perspectives on the New Age*. Albany, N.Y.: State University of New York Press.

Oosthuizen, Gerhardus C. 1992. 'The "Newness" of the New Age in South Africa and Reactions to It'. In: James R. Lewis and J. Gordon Melton (eds.), *Perspectives on the New Age*. Albany, N.Y.: State University of New York Press.

Roman, Sanaya 1986. *Personal Power Through Awareness: A Guidebook for Sensitive People*, Tiburon, Calif.: H.J. Kramer.

CHAPTER 2

Globalization or Westernization? New Age as a Contemporary Transnational Culture

Liselotte Frisk

Introduction

Globalization is a phenomenon firmly linked to *communication*, which today is worldwide and increasingly dense. People, cultures, societies, and civilizations that previously were more or less isolated from one another are now in regular contact.[1] The world has become one network of social relationships, and between its different regions there is a flow of meanings as well as of people and goods.[2]

One particular outcome of increasing communication or globalization is the growth of cultures — or systems of shared meanings, which people from the same social group use to help interpret and make sense of the world[3] — without a clear anchorage in any one territory, *transnational cultures* or *deterritorialized cultures*. We can contrast such cultures with those that are territorially defined (in terms of, for example, nations).[4]

One of these deterritorialized transnational cultures is New Age. What we call 'New Age' (I will not discuss here the problem of definition) may look slightly different in different places around the globe, but the main characteristics are almost identical everywhere. New Age could, for example, be seen as a large-scale, decentralized

1. Beyer 1994, 2.
2. Hannertz 1997, 237.
3. Hall 1996, 176.
4. Ibid. 237-41.

religious subculture that draws its principal inspiration from sources outside of the Judeo-Christian tradition;[5] as eclectic teachings and practices centred around Self-spirituality,[6] as a transformative vision of a new world and a new human being[7] or as a smorgasbord of concepts from different cultures, with a focus on healing and multicultural methods to reach the healed condition.[8]

Transnational cultures with religious implications are not new. Buddhism, Christianity, and Islam have always been cultures with global aspirations. However, there are some interesting differences between *historical* and *contemporary* transnational cultures. This issue will be discussed in this paper, as also will be the subject of so-called *global values*. Finally, the question of whether New Age should be seen as an extension of *Western culture* or as a truly *global culture* will be addressed.

Transnational Cultures Today and Yesterday

Historically, there have often been close relations between religions and socio-cultural particularisms. Nevertheless, there have also been transnational religions with universal aspirations, like Buddhism, Christianity, and Islam, religions thus contradicting political boundaries.[9] Common to these historical religions was — and still is — the aspiration to include everyone, not excluding people because of, for example, nationality or ethnic origin.

However, there seem to be some fundamental differences between the historical global religions and New Age, differences which are related to the accelerating globalized situation. Irving Hexham and Karen Poewe, who have looked into this question, observe, for example, that new religions (and so New Age) consist of *fragments of different traditions*, while Buddhism, Christianity and Islam aim at remaining true to one consistent *world tradition*. The ideal of Buddhism, Christianity, and Islam is to spread a religious metaculture that, while

5. Lewis and Melton 1992, IX.
6. Heelas 1996, 2.
7. Melton 1988, 35-36.
8. Frisk 1997, 87-90.
9. Beyer 1994, 50.

being absorbed by local cultures, should be perfectly capable of remaining identifiable. A metaculture, according to Hexham and
Poewe, consists of a minimum of elements that are reasonably consistent and uniform and are recognizable even when the metaculture
is absorbed into cultures to become movements or denominations.[10]
In contrast, like some new religions, New Age selectively combines
aspects of many traditions to create a new culture,[11] a process surely
only possible under strongly globalized conditions. According to
Hexham and Poewe, in new religions several cultures coexist 'in the
individual experience'. Whereas the aim of including people everywhere within one distinct tradition is a Christian practice, the new re-
ligionist practice includes people for whom the coexistence of ideas
from diverse cultures, traditions and practices is an inner experience.[12]

Thus, what makes New Age differ from the historical transnational religions seems to be the accelerated eclecticism and the emphasis
on an inner experience of unity of multicultural elements. This 'open'
worldview, without too much emphasis on ideas or belief systems,
has become more attractive as the plausibility of the traditional religious metacultures has been increasingly undermined. In the next
section, we will look at the main reasons for this.

The Process of Relativization and the So-Called Global Values

A key word for some theoreticians of globalization, for example Roland Robertson and Peter Beyer, is *relativization*. Globalization sets
particular societies in a wider system of societies, finally resulting in
the relativization of both societies and individuals. In a globalized
context, the norms and values institutionalized within a particular
society face the different images of the 'good society' presented by
other societies in the world.[13] The global social reality relativizes all
particular cultures, including of course the religions that form part of

10. Hexham and Poewe 1997, 42-43.
11. Ibid., 41.
12. Ibid., 46-47.
13. Beyer 1994, 26-27.

these cultures.[14] Individuals form their religious identity in the knowledge that their religion is only one among several possibilities.[15] In contemporary society, the process of relativization is what undermines the plausibility of the traditional religious metacultures. The process of relativization, according to Beyer, gives rise to the dual process of search for, on the one hand, *particularistic* identities, and on the other hand *universalistic* identities,[16] a process which is also expressed religiously.

But the process of relativization, according to Beyer, also has further implications for ideology and values related to questions of *inclusion* and *exclusion*, or ingroup/outgroup identity. In pre-modern societies, according to Beyer, the close association between moral codes, group membership, and religion structured inter-group or inter-societal relations. In situations where one societal group threatened another, or where there was simply competition, the enemy could be interpreted as the embodiment of evil, or as the negation of the correct relationship between social order and the transcendent that one's group represented. In traditional Christian theology, a person who is — morally and religiously — the Other can be legitimately seen as an apostate, an outcast. Historically, for example, Jews and barbarians were such objects of violent persecution or war. Such outsiders could become insiders only by religious conversion.[17]

Beyer claims that modern/global society (thanks to communication and relativization) has no outsiders who can serve as the social representatives of evil, danger, or chaos. Without these, the forces of order and good also become more difficult to identify at the level of global society as a whole, undermining or relativizing, for instance, moral codes.[18] Today, the globalizing tendencies of society have radically altered the conditions under which the moralizing solution is possible because the societal group now includes everyone. The person who used to be the outsider is now a neighbour. The outside/inside distinction for reinforcing the internal moral codes of societies

14. Ibid., 9.
15. Ibid., 30.
16. Loc. cit.
17. Ibid., 84-85.
18. Ibid., 72.

becomes difficult to maintain in a world of virtually instant global communication.[19]

According to Beyer, under globalized conditions there are two main responses for religion: the *conservative* option, which reasserts the reality of the devil (and persons/cultures who are seen as outsiders or evil), and the *liberal* option which dissolves the devil. According to the liberal option, even though there is evil in the world, it cannot be clearly localized or personified. And evil is especially not to be found in the existence of pluralism, including religious pluralism. Intolerance and particularistic ascription are seen as prime sources of evil. Accordingly, liberal religion is ecumenical and tolerant, and more or less agrees that there are comparable possibilities for enlightenment and salvation in different religions. The possibility of salvation, enlightenment or wisdom is for all, everyone is included. Liberal religion works for the fuller inclusion of all people in the benefits of the global community. Thus, globalization of society does not lead mainly to the death of God, but to the death of the devil.[20]

Beyer emphasizes the fact that liberal religion seeks to address the problems engendered by the global system, but on the *basis of the prevailing global values* and not in opposition to them.[21] Liberal religion thus correlates with the structural tendencies of a global society. Beyer says that the liberal option might be seen as the trend of the future. However, as for now there is also the conservative option, the reassertion of the tradition in spite of modernity, as another vital aspect of globalization. Conservative religion dichotomizes the world into the religiously pure and impure, into us and them.[22]

In many respects New Age could be seen, in the terminology of Beyer, as a liberal religion, mainly expressing the global values of inclusion, tolerance and death of the devil. Prevalent in New Age is often a kind of monistic worldview, where good and evil are not seen as absolute opposites but as relativistic parts of one reality.[23] A system like this is less inclined towards exclusion and intolerance than

19. Ibid., 85.
20. Ibid., 86-88.
21. Ibid., 104.
22. Ibid., 90-92.
23. Christensen 1996, 15.

dualistic systems. Often, New Age people could be inclusive to an extent not appreciated by everyone included. For example, I have met clergymen from the Swedish Church, who complain that they do not know what to do with certain New Age people in their parish, because they see no conflicts between the teachings of the church and New Age, and, for example, insist on adding 'pagan' rituals or 'pagan' songs to funerals.

New Age would thus correlate with the structural tendencies of a global society, and therefore, according to Beyer, is part of the liberal type of religion that he sees as the trend of the future. However, this conclusion could well be discussed. According to Hexham and Poewe, tolerance and inclusion in new religions is nothing but a chimera.[24] If there are insiders in a social group, there are always outsiders also. Any identity is based on differentiation from others,[25] although boundaries could of course be more or less well defined, and are probably less so in for example, New Age, than in some other social groups. In New Age the image of 'the Other', the Outsider, is often seen as the one 'not so developed spiritually'. For example, in texts such as *The Celestine Prophecy* and *The Tenth Insight,* the Other is represented by Priests and Scientists,[26] an image of evil which is not really uncommon in New Age-culture.[27] New Age practitioners certainly mix elements from different cultures in their own worldview and practice, and are often tolerant of others choosing other mixtures. But still, this openness is not as open as it may seem. What may be included in New Age is highly selective, certainly including many things, but also excluding some things. As Olav Hammer observes, there are only certain mixtures of cultural elements in circulation in New Age, excluding other mixtures.[28] In the next section, I will discuss the kind of cultural elements circulating in New Age, as well as mention the ones *not* circulating, which is an interesting question in itself.

Personally, I think it might also be worthwhile to discuss Beyer's

24. Hexham and Poewe 1997, 46-47.
25. Massey 1995, 67.
26. Hammer 1997, 281-282.
27. Heelas 1996, 18-19.
28. Hammer 1997, 20-21.

view of 'global values' as the natural outcome of globalization and the trend of the future. The reason is that the so-called 'global values' are closely connected to Western secular core values like freedom, equality, and democracy, deriving from the Enlightenment world-view and the ideals of the French Revolution.[29] Is the whole global-ization discussion perhaps (once more) an expression of Western eth-nocentrism, where, for example, it is more than natural to see 'pluralism' as 'good' and 'the future of tomorrow'? Could the defin-ing of so-called 'global values' be seen as a kind of 'Orientalism', where one contrasts Oriental vices (for example Muslim fundamen-talism) to Western virtues, like pluralism and tolerance?[30] If 'global values' are identical with 'Western values', surely the whole global-ization discussion could be seen in a new perspective.

Globalization or Westernization?

Globalization theories agree that modernization in the West has di-rectly resulted in the spread of certain vital institutions of Western modernization to the rest of the globe, especially the modern capital-ist economy, the nation-state, and scientific rationality in the form of modern technology.

Peter Beyer describes the historical development of globalization as a mutual development of economic, religious, legal, political, and scientific progress.[31] Western expansion (in all areas) was, according to Beyer, a direct result of the shift in European society to a primacy of *functionally specialized societal subsystems*. The more powerful com-municative capacity of these systems enabled their global spread. At least until the late nineteenth or early twentieth century, however, people who almost exclusively were culturally Western carried out the expansion of these systems. Until that time, it was reasonable for all involved and affected to see the process as the spread of Western socio-cultural particularism, of Western civilization. Adopting West-ern-bred technique seemed inseparable from becoming a Westerner

29. Appadurai 1997, 299; Beyer 1994, 100-1.
30. Rose 1995, 93-95.
31. Beyer 1994, 52.

in all aspects of life. Globalization therefore meant and, in some respects, still means Westernization. But, according to Beyer, this process ran into important obstacles. The increased power of the functional system derived both from their specialization and the prevalence within them of *cognitively oriented structures* — they emphasized instrumental rationality. In the sphere of religion, the rise of liberal and ecumenical theologies points to expectation structures that stress learning instead of unchanging norms. For a time it may have seemed that the global spread of the Western-bred systems meant dissemination of Western normative particularism. But, as stated by Beyer, in the end the spread of cognitively oriented structures also undermined the privileged position of Western 'tradition' not only in the non-Western world, but also in the West.[32]

Therefore, Beyer argues forcefully — and others with him — that although key globalizing structures originated in the West, globalization is not just another word for Western expansion. Globalization is more than the spread of one historically existing culture at the expense of all others. It is the creation of a new global culture, one that increasingly becomes the broader social context of all particular cultures in the world, including those of the West. The spread of the global social reality therefore occurs quite as much at the cost of the latter as of non-Western cultures. *All* cultures change dramatically in the process.[33]

Still, the discussion as to what extent globalization implies cultural homogenization and cultural heterogenization, and the role of the Western culture in these processes, continues. According to Arjun Appadurai, there are many empirical facts supporting the homogenization argument. Often, he says, the homogenization argument is complemented by an argument about Americanization. However, he critizes this argument, partly because all influences are not American, and partly because forces brought into new societies tend to become indigenized one way or the other.[34]

Some theoreticians attempt to apply a *power perspective* to globalization. One of them is Doreen Massey, who discusses the power re-

32. Ibid., 53-54.
33. Ibid., 8-9.
34. Appadurai 1997, 295.

lations between 'centre' and 'periphery' regarding different areas (like economy, politics, media) and different places. For example, in the case of media, she says that a few major corporations dominate the transmission of news and thus, very often, a particular first world understanding of it. While there are increasing mixtures of cultures in all parts of the world, the directions of this mixing are unequal. For example, people in London may go to an exhibition to learn something about Papua New Guinea. But people in Papua New Guinea do not have to go to an exhibition to learn about Western culture. Their world is already framed by it.[35] Although not all cultural flows run in the same direction, many observers point out that it is clear there are still broad systematic lines and directions: from 'West' to 'rest', from the United States of America to other first world societies, from global cities outwards.[36] The social anthropologist Ulf Hannertz remarks that transnational cultures are on the whole usually more marked by some territorial culture than by others. Most of them are, according to him, in different ways extensions or transformations of the cultures of western Europe and North America, and are organized so as to make people from western Europe and North America feel as much at home as possible (by using their own languages, for one thing).[37]

In many respects, this is also valid for New Age. The *lingua franca* of New Age is English also outside English-speaking countries, a fact so natural that it is no longer even commented upon in information pamphlets on New Age-related lectures and courses. And that the flow from the US of New Age books and New Age charismatic leaders is rather a one-way flow is easily seen.

However, there are also of course many non-Western traits prevalent in New Age, as the characteristic feature of New Age is precisely the multi-cultural mixture. Except for Western esotericism and Western psychological components, the most eminent components in New Age could be said to derive from Eastern religion and some native cultures, mainly American Indian ones. The fact that some non-Western cultures are influential in New Age does not, however,

35. Massey 1995, 70.
36. Ibid., 71.
37. Hannertz 1997, 244.

really change the main direction of cultural flow and cultural power. As people in London go to an exhibition to learn about Papua New Guinea, or even travel as a tourist to New Guinea (a possibility brought about by the effect of globalization and an important fact in itself), New Age-practitioners may go on sacred journeys to India, or may adopt new-schamanistic techniques. But it does not change the main direction of cultural flow, not much more than the exhibition on Papua New Guinea changes the culture in London. Perhaps selected traits from non-Western cultures could rather be said to have a *supporting* effect on Western cultural values in New Age. For example, the Western value of Self-spirituality, individualism and experience-orientation, could find support in some parts of Eastern religion (in the sense of The Sacred as being something inside the human being, not outside). But the metavalues of New Age seem otherwise mainly to have a firm base in Western culture.

What could also be discussed in this context is the *absence* of the influence of certain cultures in New Age. African cultures are, for example, almost completely absent, as are Muslim cultures also to a high degree. New Age is a global mixture of different cultural elements, but still some elements and some specific mixtures are missing. This fact might also say something about the directions of cultural flow in the global society.

What the situation will be in the future we do not know. There are clearly 'reverse' cultural flows under contemporary globalized conditions. But still, I think, there will always be some people and cultures more in charge than others; some have the power to initiate flows and movements, others don't. And at the moment, this initiative is still in the West, not only in connection with New Age.

Bibliography

Appadurai, A. 1997. 'Disjuncture and Difference in the Global Cultural Economy'. In: M. Featherstone (ed.), *Global Culture. Nationalism, Globalization and Modernity*. London: Sage, 295-310.

Beyer, P. 1994. *Religion and Globalization*. London: Sage.

Christensen, L.D. 1996. *New Age etik. Ledende New Age-forfatteres holdninger til social- og miljopolitiske sporgsmål*. Copenhagen: Gyldendal.

Frisk, L. 1997. 'Vad är New Age? Centrala begrepp och historiska rötter', *SRÅ* vol. 6, 87-97.

Hall, S. 1995. 'New Cultures for Old'. In: D. Massey and P. Jess (eds.), *A Place in the World? Places, Cultures and Globalization*. Oxford: The Open University, 175-213.

Hammer, O. 1997. *På spaning efter helheten. New Age — en ny folktro?* Stockholm: Wahlström & Widstrand.

Hannertz, U. 1997. 'Cosmopolitans and Locals in World Culture'. In: M. Featherstone (ed.), *Global Culture. Nationalism, Globalization and Modernity*. London: Sage. 237-51.

Heelas, P. 1996. *The New Age Movement. The Celebration of the Self and the Sacralization of Modernity*. Oxford: Blackwell.

Hexham, I. and K. Poewe 1997. *New Religions as Global Cultures. Making the Human Sacred*. Oxford: Westview.

Lewis, J.P. and J.G. Melton 1992. 'Introduction'. In: J.P. Lewis and J. G. Melton (eds.), *Perspectives on the New Age*. Albany: State University of New York Press, ix-xii.

Massey, D. 1995. 'The Conceptualization of Place'. In: D. Massey and P. Jess (eds.), *A Place in the World? Places, Cultures and Globalization*. Oxford: The Open University, 45-85.

Melton, J.G. 1988. 'A History of the New Age Movement'. In: R. Basil (ed.), *Not Necessarily the New Age. Critical Essays*. Buffalo, New York: Prometheus Books, 35-53.

Rose, G. 1995. 'Place and Identity: A Sense of Place'. In: D. Massey and P. Jess (eds.), *A Place in the World? Places, Cultures and Globalization*. Oxford: The Open University, 87-132.

CHAPTER 3

Same Message from Everywhere: The Sources of Modern Revelation

Olav Hammer

Prolegomenon

With complete confidence in her interpretation, intuitive healer and best-selling author Caroline Myss claims that the second chakra is connected with the kabbalistic principle Yesod, the Catholic sacrament of the communion, male energies, the forces of electromagnetism, our relationship with God and the distinction between yin and yang.[1] The present paper is concerned with this universalizing hermeneutics. What enables Myss to say something that departs so radically from conventional historiography, and yet presumably convince a wide readership?

However, before entering into the empirical details of New Age beliefs and their esoteric precursors, I feel compelled to begin this paper with some theoretical preliminaries.

Which Globalization?

Globalization is, to quote one of the seminal papers on the subject, the fact that 'the world is rapidly coming to be apprehended as "one place", that is, as a totality wherein discrete selves, nation-states, and even civilization traditions have their respective niches, each interconnected by complex, reticular relationships of belligerence and beneficence, competition and compromise, discordance and détente'.[2]

1. Myss 1996, 129 ff.
2. Robertson and Garrett 1991, ix, f.

Cultural elements have of course always been transported across geographical distances and have been incorporated among other groups than those who created these elements. The transformation leading to our own time is one of degree rather than essence. Yet, the scope of contact and the rapidity of influence make it reasonable to see our own time as one of unprecedented globalization. The rise of a mass culture, the development of electronic media, the emergence of more efficient systems for the distribution of goods and the increased movement of people across national borders have resulted in a large-scale interaction of cultures.

When considering the intersection of these elements of globalization with the phenomena of modern religiosity, especially of the New Age type, some distinctions are in order.

Firstly, cultural globalization is not one single thing, but a common name for several distinct processes. A first distinction can be made between the *production*, the *consumption* and the *distribution* of religious elements.

The element of global distribution is linked with the objective transnational processes that constitute one of the central elements of the paradigm of globalization. Thus, the highly successful marketing of American New Age literature is a particularly visible facet of the global distribution of religious products.

Globalized consumption of cultural elements in part has to do with a shift in *communitas*. Whereas geographical borders bound older imagined communities — the nation state would be a prime example — newer communities have become increasingly divorced from such geographically definable contexts. Thus, a Californian with a passionate interest in UFO channelling might feel a much stronger bond of sympathy with a British or Swedish UFO enthusiast than with his Southern Baptist neighbour.

Here, however, I will be primarily concerned with the third facet of globalization: the production of religious elements. In particular, this paper will be concerned with globalized religious production as objectified in modern esoteric texts.[3] The globalization of religious

3. The term 'modern esoteric texts' is here stipulatively defined as texts written by spokespersons of movements with at least partial roots in theosophy.

production concerns the fact that such esoteric texts in general, and New Age texts in particular, make overt use of a variety of historical epochs and more or less exotic cultures. These purported sources of spiritual wisdom are used as the significant Others in identity construction work.[4] Thus, in contrast with the objective structures involved in global distribution, production is intimately linked with the second central element of the globalization paradigm, namely the subjective awareness of the variety of other cultures.

Terminology

The concept of globalization is by preference in the theoretical literature linked with the emergence of post-modernity. Several themes of the discourse on the post-modern condition will be readily recognizable in the pages to follow. Thus, New Age doctrines can function as pastiches in the narrow, technical sense of the word: a kind of imitation of other styles or discourses without the awareness that what one represents is an imitation. To the extent, however, that this paper concerns the development of collective identities based on the appropriation of exotic Others, the vocabulary of postmodern theory in all its varieties is perhaps not the most fruitful. Fredric Jameson remarks that a crucial component of the post-modern condition is the demise of the conception of a unique self and a private identity.[5] On the contrary, the belief in the existence of a core or true Self is a recurring theme in New Age texts. The appropriation of shamanistic techniques and the creation of pastiches on Indian philosophies are part of an attempt to bring out that core Self from behind the dross of the false ego.

In order to discuss globalization and the production of religious elements, I would like to turn to a different theoretical understanding of the phases of modernity, namely the work of Anthony Giddens.

4. The term significant Others was coined by George Herbert Meade in the 1930's and has been used in the theory of personality development. Here, the concept is metaphorically extended to the process whereby spokespersons for a given religious position construct the identities of their doctrines in relation to abstract or concrete Others.
5. Jameson 1983, 114.

Giddens' historiography rests on a view of modernity as radically discontinuous with earlier social forms.[6] The characteristics of modernity, understood as a series of social, institutional and cultural formations that have their roots in seventeenth century Western society, have according to Giddens been radicalized during recent decades. Among these characteristics, one finds factors such as the pace and scope of change, and the rise of new social institutions such as the nation-state. Based on this conception, he has formulated a terminology for the analysis of late modernity.[7]

The *separation of time and space* entails an abstract view of space and of time. Spatial separation decreases in importance, as it becomes possible to enter into relations of various kinds with physically absent or distant Others. Similarly, the time-line of late modernity is divorced from the lived experience of individuals. References are possible to periods of past or future time that are entirely abstracted from everyday life. Thus, the time-line of the modern esoteric tradition does indeed encompass a mythical history with little direct relevance to the here-and-now of the individual adherent of esoteric belief systems. One might argue that this mythic history has deeper roots in the intellectual history of the West. The characteristics of late modernity could then be said to manifest themselves in the *scope* of cultures and epochs that are pre-empted by the narratives based on this time-line.

Related to the separation of time and space is the concept of *disembedding*, defined by Giddens as the separation of locally grounded relations and their transposition to entirely new contexts. This characteristic of late modernity is obviously related to the concept of globalization. Whereas elements of a local, traditional culture might be *dis*embedded and transposed into a neighbouring locality, modern communications make it feasible to *dis*embed elements of Indian, Chinese or Native American origin and *re*embed them in a Western context, thereby giving these elements new functions and new meanings.

6. Giddens' terminology seems usable also in a historiography that sees changes rather than radical discontinuities between traditional and modern societies. The brief summary given here thus implies no commitment to any particular view of the rise of modernity.
7. Giddens 1991; Giddens 1990, esp. 17 ff.

Connected with this radical removal of social and cultural constructions from their immediate contexts is the concept of *trust* or *faith* in experts. In the specific case of the disembedding of cultural elements, the entrepreneurs who instigate processes of disembedding and who disseminate their radically recontextualized versions of how these cultural elements should be understood, function as experts of sorts. In order to accept the new narratives, one needs faith in their veracity, and not hermeneutic suspicion.

What, then, are these 'relations of various kinds with physically absent or distant Others' that are established through the process of disembedding? Going one step beyond Giddens' terminology, disembedding can be seen to result in a variety of new cultural products, along a spectrum. At one end lie new cultural products that I propose to call structurally conservative. A characteristic example might be stock exchanges in New York, Stockholm and Tokyo, where a truly internationalized set of economic processes is expressed with relatively marginal local adaptations. The verbal expressions, body language and social norms accepted by the actors on the stock exchange are locally grounded, yet the fundamental structures, the financial transactions themselves, are based on globally recognized rules.

At the other end of the spectrum one finds structurally radical cultural products. Examples here might be the custom of many tourists to wear local clothing, without any awareness of the cultural codes permeating the choice of clothing. A male backpacker might crisscross Guatemala and unknown to himself cause considerable hilarity by wearing Guatemalan women's blouses. Here, the surface characteristics of the disembedded cultural product — the specific articles of clothing worn by the backpacker — are retained. The fundamental structures — the ethnic and gender codes expressed by wearing Guatemalan women's blouses — are disregarded.

Where on this spectrum can we place religious disembedding, as we can observe it in the fundamental texts of esoteric spokespersons? A cursory reading of such texts gives rise to the suspicion that we are witnessing a massive process of structurally radical disembedding. Already a century ago, the ideologists of the Theosophical Society juxtaposed elements from the most diverse sources. An example, taken more or less at random, is the following quote from Charles

Leadbeater's attempt to explain the rationale behind the crucifixion of Jesus:

> Now this great sacrifice — the descent of the Second Logos into matter in the form of monadic essence — was somewhat elaborately set forth in symbol in the ritual of the Egyptian form of the Sotâpatti initiation, and, as before stated, the Christ had frequently used a description of the exoteric side of its ceremonies to illustrate and emphasize his teaching on the subject […]. The formula, handed down to the Egyptians from the exponents of Atlantean magic in far distant ages, ran thus: […].[8]

In just a few lines of text, Leadbeater manages to combine a concept from neo-platonism, a philosophical term from Leibniz, belief in the fabled continent of Atlantis and assorted references to India, Egypt and Christianity.

This tendency remains throughout the post-theosophical religious positions up to the New Age writings of our own time. The remainder of this paper will address the question of how this is done.

Eclecticism — To a Point

Eric Klein is a minor celebrity within one burgeoning subculture of the New Age, viz. groups who continue to speculate on a coming evolutionary jump, a New Age *senso strictu* to use the terminology of Wouter Hanegraaff. Mankind, we learn, is on the verge of ascending in consciousness from a three-dimensional to a higher-dimensional mode of existence. This obviously scientistic metaphor of evolution is attributed to four sources: Jesus, Ashtar, the archangel Michael and St. Germain.

What we can note is firstly; that each of the four purported sources of information is originally connected with its own tradition:

Jesus, who is obviously connected with Christianity, has been a staple of unorthodox thought throughout the history of the Western esoteric tradition.

---

8. Leadbeater 1904, 62 f.

Ashtar entered occult lore in the early days of UFO channelling. In or around 1952, George Van Tassel, former aircraft inspector for the Lockheed Company, began weekly Friday-night channelling of UFO inhabitants.[9] Ashtar entered history in 1952. In van Tassel's book *I Rode A Flying Saucer*, a channelling dated July 18 lets this being present himself with the words 'Hail to you beings of Shan. I greet you in love and peace. My identity is Ashtar, commandant quadra sector, patrol station Schare, all projections, all waves. Greetings'. Ashtar continued to transmit messages throughout the fall of that year, reprimanding humanity on its use of uranium to construct bombs and promising to assist us in following a better path. Since then, Ashtar has advanced to becoming the chief of an entire host of space beings, and various members of the Ashtar Command are channelled by individuals around the globe.

Michael is the most difficult to trace, but has been a staple of the esoteric tradition at least since a 16th century tract on occult history, Johannes Trithemius' *De septem secundeis*, was translated in the late 19th century. Anna Kingsford, Rudolf Steiner and a host of channellers ascribe their teachings to him. Thus the Archangel Michael is a syncretistic figure well before his appropriation by New Age writers.

Saint Germain was a flesh-and-blood occultist of the 18th century, entered the theosophical pantheon around the turn of the 20th century and became a major figure in the mythology of several American post-theosophical offshoots, most notably the *I AM* religious activity and the Church Universal and Triumphant.

One can in Eric Klein's text note how the modern esoteric tradition makes use of two fundamentally different strategies of creating an *emic* historiography: reinterpretation and creation. Some parts build on radically reinterpreted but actually existing traditions. Obviously, neither Jesus nor the Archangel Michael were innovations created by

---

9. *Fortean Times*, issue 118, available on-line at: www.forteantimes.com/artic/118/rock.html. All web sites quoted were active in January 2000. An apologetic description of the early contactee era can be found at the official site of the movement centred on van Tassel's channellings at: www.georgevantassel.com

Western esotericisms. The Ashtar Command, on the other hand, is constructed in modern times and there is no pre-existing tradition to reinterpret.

These two fundamental modes of inventing a tradition recur throughout the vast corpus of New Age material. Spurious sources such as Atlantis coexist with radically reinterpreted ones such as Buddhism or Shamanism.

Culturally Relevant Sources

The ancient civilizations and native peoples referred to by texts attempting to legitimize these rituals thus range from Atlantis and Lemuria to Tibet and Japan. Other New Age rituals and beliefs would invoke an even more eclectic list of 'wisdom traditions': the China of alternative medicine, the Native Americans of neo-shamanism, the Australian aborigines of Marlo Morgan, Celtic druids and kabbalists, not to mention extraterrestrials and dolphins.

Each new purported source from which the modern esoteric tradition has disembedded elements was part of the current cultural landscape of the West at the time these cultures were invoked. Theosophy appropriated Atlantis from other esotericisms, Lemuria from the writings of Ernst Haeckel, Egypt from the French occultists, India from what has been called the Oriental renaissance, and so forth.

From theosophy and onwards, basically the same core set of exotic cultures has been appropriated by each of the various esoteric positions, while the precise roles that these cultures play within each position differs. The differences rarely seem to be motivated by any lesser or greater reliance on actual elements culled from, say, Egypt, India or Tibet. Rather, each position comprises a ready historiographic template into which the various cultures are fitted. Earlier positions, notably those of Blavatsky, Leadbeater and Steiner were based on grand narratives in which Egypt or Atlantis, e.g., played clearly delimited roles. More recent positions, e.g. the readings of Edgar Cayce, present more fragmented myths. Various New Age writers reduce the role of these significant cultures to being a source of particular doctrinal elements.

Thus, esoteric texts are engaged in the construction of an *emic* historiography. What is perhaps most striking is the fact that *emic* and *etic* historiography tend to move apart, despite the ready availability of mainstream or *etic* histories. Thus, New Age writers do not necessarily see older generations of esoteric writers as their spiritual forebears. A century ago, this was still largely the case.

Henry Olcott, co-founder with Helena Blavatsky of the Theosophical Society, constructed such a lineage in his first presidential address, in which he referred to Albertus Magnus, Alfarabi, Roger Bacon, Cagliostro, Pico della Mirandola, Robert Fludd, Paracelsus, Cornelius Agrippa, Henry More, the Chaldeans, kabbalists, Egyptians, hermeticists, alchemists and Rosicrucians.[10] V.S. Solovyoff, one of Blavatsky's earliest biographers, refers to one of her letters in which she traces the theosophical idea back to the Jewish and Egyptian kabbalah, to hermetic philosophy, Paracelsus and Reichenbach.[11] Neither Blavatsky nor Olcott at this early stage ventured beyond the ancient Near East in their quest for roots. Both presented their teachings as the latest offshoot of a long line of esoteric belief systems, a view that lies close to the scholarly understanding of the place of theosophy in Western intellectual history.

The New Age literature of the late twentieth century has largely abandoned this view of history. Bestselling literature in this genre places by preference the origins of its doctrines either in the distant East or among native peoples. With the passing of time, the esoteric tradition would thus seem to have been a locus of massive globalization. The trend towards seeing non-European religious traditions as one's positive Others lies at the very centre of the construction of a New Age tradition.

Stages of Appropriation

The brief introduction to Eric Klein reveals the underlying presupposition of much of the disembedding that takes place. His four purported sources are made to reveal the same message of a coming evolutionary leap in the history of mankind. When entirely imaginary cultures are invoked to support a given claim, this is, technically

10. Quoted in Prothero 1996, 50 f.
11. Solovyoff 1895, 256 ff.

speaking, hardly a problem. Ancient Lemurians or the space brothers can be made to say anything the esoteric spokesperson would like them to say. Actually existing religious traditions may prove more recalcitrant. How does one go about making various positive Others conform to pre-existing expectations?

The historical process by which such an appropriation takes place commonly follows distinct stages. First, travel narratives are published, or ethnographic or historical accounts become available, in which the exotic custom is presented. It is not meant, however, that the descriptions in such works should be emulated directly by a Western audience. Creative spokespersons for the esoteric tradition read such works and transform them to fit in with culturally predetermined elements of their own (Western) tradition. Then come the first do-it-yourself books, works that transform the new element from a belief to be accepted to a practice to be performed or an experience to be sought after. Knowledge that was previously difficult to gain now becomes increasingly available to a general readership. Commonly, a small number of esoteric interpretations become trendsetting templates that structure the doctrines propounded in later works.

The rapid process of reinterpretation and change soon transforms the originally exotic doctrine into an organic part of the new context. Neo-shamanism as practiced by Michael Harner's students differs significantly from the tribal shamanism of Harner's informants amid the Shuar and Conibo indians. Sufism in the West is something quite different from the Sufism of the Mourids of Senegal, for example. And the kabbalah of the occult revival is distinct from the complex kabbalism of medieval Spain. Writers will attempt to stress continuity and disregard change, a legitimizing process that has its typical elements.

Strategies of Appropriation

The basic legitimizing strategy underlying this stage-by-stage appropriation we can call *pattern recognition*. This is the mechanism that highlights any similarities to the exclusion of differences. Terms from different traditions are declared to be essentially synonymous. Rituals that share overt characteristics are said to be more or less iden-

tical. Two or more doctrinal elements that bear even the faintest similarity are subsumed under the same heading.

The repertoire of mankind's religious creativity is vast but not
limitless. There are just so many basic themes available to those who
wish to speculate on, for example, life after death. Death can be the
end of everything; we can be transported into some transcendent
realm; there is the idea of resurrection; or we can return to a new life.
The more one looks at the structures, interpretations, ideological uses
and narrative details of the various speculations on life after death,
the more they appear to be unique. Hindu reincarnation is not the
same as kabbalistic reincarnation. Among the kabbalists, Isaac Luria
has a very different conception of reincarnation than does the anony-
mous author of the Zohar.

However, for a synthesizing mind intent on finding a perennial
philosophy underlying the divergent traditions, there is ample material from which to synthesize, and every opportunity to claim that the
divergences are insignificant details. Esoteric authors from Helena
Blavatsky to James Redfield can proclaim that all spiritual traditions
have included the concept of reincarnation, in the singular.

In fact, the need to force incompatible religious traditions into a
pre-established mould even gives rise to modern legends. Thus, the
lack of reincarnation doctrines in mainstream Christianity has produced one of the most robust legends of the esoteric tradition. Briefly stated, this legend claims that the earliest Christian communities
once taught the doctrine of reincarnation, but that the powerful dig-
nitaries of the church have hidden this fact from ordinary believers.

The story of Christian reincarnation is found in theosophical writings from the late 19th century, in the readings of Edgar Cayce and in
the literature of various American post-theosophical movements. It is
even today retold in numerous New Age books. Hanegraaff has followed the legend as far as to the writings of Shirley Maclaine, who
added a new twist to it by confusing the council at Constantinople
with the council in Nicaea.[12] Books more recent than those in
Hanegraaff's corpus continue to reproduce the legend. Thus hypno-

---

12. Hanegraaff 1998, 321 f. briefly surveys the occurrences in New Age liter-
    ature of this legend.

therapist Brian L. Weiss claims that his research into the origins of re-incarnation beliefs have shown how the doctrine was considered de-stabilizing by the worldly authorities under the emperor Constantine and was therefore banned in the sixth century.[13]

Universal Healing?

In order to bring together all the points discussed so far, I would like to introduce an example that builds on reinterpretation as well as invention, on pattern recognition among rituals as well as synonymization of terminology. This example consists of a family of historically related healing rituals, involving the laying on of hands.

Arguably one of the 'oriental' elements most obviously part of a New Age worldview is Reiki healing. Reiki was popularized in the West by Hawayo Takata, a woman of Japanese descent born in Hawaii. In Reiki literature Mrs Takata's lineage is traced back to Japan to the person of Mikao Usui, of whom, however, few verifiable biographical data are available.

According to a widespread founding legend, Usui had an ardent wish as a Christian convert to be able to perform healing miracles of the kind reported in the New Testament, and was rewarded by receiving knowledge of Reiki healing from various sources, including otherwise unknown Tibetan texts and a visionary experience on a mountain near his home town of Kyoto. In the thoroughly eclectic fashion typical of many New Age elements, books on Reiki can also note that this form of healing transmits a form of universal life energy to the chakras, force centres purportedly known to 'most eastern philosophies'.[14] Etic historiography is only able to trace Reiki, in the form practiced today, to Mrs Takata, although there does seem to be a Japanese form of Reiki transmitted through a different lineage. Reiki began to spread throughout the West around 1980.

13. Weiss 1992, ch. 3; Weiss' own quoted source is a book by two authors with roots in the theosophical movement, Cranston and Head 1986.
14. Arjava Petter 1998, 100.

At the time of writing, two decades later, there is a truly amazing variety of healing systems all claiming to be part of the tradition of Reiki healing. Beside the lineage most commonly practiced in the West, there are practitioners claiming a more genuine Japanese tradition, who call their method Traditional Japanese Reiki.[15] There are varieties that can be traced back to one of the few Japanese students taught by Mrs Takata.[16] There are Egyptianizing forms.[17] There are Tibetanizing varieties.[18] There are several forms of Reiki that have added or deleted elements of the lineages from which they stem due to psychic information purportedly given by a variety of spirit guides.[19] There are forms of Reiki claimed to come from Atlantis or Lemuria.[20] There are forms that include belief in the Ascended Masters of theosophy.[21] And there are forms that freely mix several or all of the above.[22]

One example from this family of rituals will show how truly unorthodox emic historiography can be. Ancient Egyptian roots are claimed for a method of ritual healing similar to Reiki, called Sekhem, which in the light of conventional historiography appears to date back no further than 1984. Sekhem was created by Patrick Ziegler. Ziegler is said to have stayed overnight in a pyramid, and 'experienced many initiations including an electric blue-white ball of

---

15. See web site: www.japanese-reiki.org16. Raku Kei Reiki, see web site: www.sacredpath.org/html/reiki/general/orighandkanji.htm
16. Raku Kei Reiki, see web site: www.sacredpath.org/html/reiki/general/orighandkanji.htm
17. Sekhem, see web site: www.geocities.com/HotSprings/5985/aEgoddess.htm
18. Several forms of healing claim to be Tibetan versions of Reiki, see web site: www.geocities.com/HotSprings/9434/branches1.html#Tibetan
19. Tera Mai Reiki: see web site: www.ozemail.com.au/~teramai/kathleen.html
20. Stein 1995; See also statement by Helen Belot on web site: www.geocities.com/HotSprings/5985/aEgoddess.htm
21. Reiki Plus®: see web site: www.reikiplus.com/what_is_reikiplus.html
22. Among these one finds Usui Tibetan Reiki, see web site: angelreiki.nu/level3/tibetan.htm; Sacred Path Reiki, see web site: www.sacredpath.org/html/reiki/indexs/indexr.htm

light entering his heart'.[23] After returning to the United States shortly thereafter, Patrick became a Reiki Master and began practicing
Sekhem at the same time as Reiki. Two of Ziegler's students, Kathleen McMasters and Tom Seamon, developed a full set of seven initiatory levels known as 'attunements', effectively formalizing the first of
several schools of Sekhem healing as practiced at the time of writing.
Although the method was received through revelation, connections
with Egypt are claimed in that the word *skhm* supposedly is an Ancient Egyptian synonym of Chinese *qi* or Sanskrit *prana*.

A similar synonymization wields its homogenizing influence over
the entire religious terminology of Reiki, supporting the claim that
the revelation received by Mikao Usui on that mountain in Japan was
identical to every other true healing system known to mankind since
time immemorial. An example of synonymization at work is the following passage from *Essential Reiki* by Diane Stein:

> The living body, human or animal, radiates warmth and energy. This energy
> is the life force itself, and has as many names as there are human civiliz-
> ations[…] The Polynesian Hunas call this healing force *Mana*, and the Native
> American Iroquois people call it *Orenda*. It is known as *Prana* in India, *Ruach*
> in Hebrew, *Barraka* in the Islamic countries and *Ch'i* in China. Some individ-
> ual healers have termed it *Orgone Energy* (Wilhelm Reich), *Animal Magnetism*
> (Franz Mesmer), and *Archaeus* (Paracelsus). In Japan the energy is termed *Ki*
> and it is from this word that Reiki is named.[24]

With synonymization we return to the trust in experts that Giddens
holds to be inextricably linked to the process of disembedding. Synonymization plays on the curious double role of words in a foreign
language interspersed in a text written, for example, in English. As in
ethnographic accounts or travel writing, the exotic terminology gives
an air of authenticity to the text, a hint that the author is cognizant
with the writings of an exotic culture, or at least with a specialized
and arcane vocabulary that is not accessible to the layperson. At the

23. Patrick Ziegler's initiatory ordeals are described on the web site:
    www.wholeliving.com/BR-Online/1998/122/sekhem/sekhem.html
24. Stein 1995, 16.

same time, the sheer incomprehensibility and untranslateability of the terminology ensures that the reader will have little choice but to accept the interpretations of the writer.[25] To what extent is it reasonable to claim that *mana* equals *prana*? The average reader has little possibility to evaluate the author's claims.

In the case of Reiki, the significant Others are little more than interchangeable tokens. For the outsider, no differentiating characteristics in these methods motivate the specific attributions to Atlantis, Egypt, Tibet or any other source.

Concluding Remarks

If the many purported origins of New Age elements are taken as signs of religious globalization, it is a globalization that has moved further and further along the structurally radical end of the spectrum. Bits and pieces of non-Western traditions are disembedded from their original religious contexts. Through an incessant bricolage carried out by leading religious virtuosi, these fragments are re-embedded in a modern, Western esoteric religious setting. The principal mechanism of doing this, is by forcing these exotic elements into a fairly rigid, pre-existing interpretive mould. Thereby, to the believer, the same message does indeed seem to come from everywhere.

Bibliography

Arjava Petter, F. 1998. *Reiki Fire*. Twin Lakes, Wisc.: Lotus Light Publications.

Cranston, S. and J. Head 1986. *Reincarnation: the Phoenix Fire Mystery*. New York: Julian Press.

Dubuisson, D. 1993. *Mythologies du XXe siècle*. Lille: Presses Universitaires de Lille.

25. This strategy is of course by no means exclusive to the modern esoteric tradition. In some cases, the use of exotic languages have been deconstructed as tendentious and actively misleading, cf. Dubuisson's harsh criticism of Eliade's translations from Sanskrit texts in Dubuisson 1993, 229.

Giddens, A. 1990. *The Consequences of Modernity.* Cambridge: Polity.

Giddens, A. 1991. *Self-Identity and Modernity.* Cambridge: Polity.

Hanegraaff, W. 1998. *New Age Religion and Western Culture.* Albany, N.Y.: Suny Press.

Jameson, F. 1983. 'Postmodernism and Consumer Culure'. In: H. Foster (ed.) *The Anti-Aesthetic: Essays on Postmodern Culture.* Port Townsend, Wash.: Bay Press.

Leadbeater, C.W. 1904. *The Christian Creed.* London: The Theosophical Publishing Society.

Myss, C. 1996. *Anatomy of the Spirit.* London: Bantam.

Prothero, S. 1996. *The White Buddhist: the Asian Odyssey of Henry Steel Olcott.* Bloomington: Indiana University Press.

Robertson, R. and W. Garrett, (eds.) 1991. *The Globalization of Religion.* New York: Paragon.

Solovyoff, V.S. 1895. *A Modern Priestess of Isis.* London: Longman Green.

Stein, D. 1995. *Essential Reiki.* Freedom, Calif.: The Crossing Press.

Weiss, B.L. 1992. *Through Time into Healing.* New York: Simon & Schuster.

CHAPTER 4

After the New Age: Is There a Next Age?

Massimo Introvigne

Introduction

Globalization and the creation of a 'global village' are now generally
recognized as categories whose implications for religion are extremely relevant (Kurtz 1995). On the other hand, while sociologists of religion were slowly applying the globalization category to their field,
a number of other labels emerged in general social theory. Among
these were 'glocalization', for a process where not only the global
becomes local, but the local in turn becomes global; and
'McDonaldization' (Ritzer 1997; Smart 1999), for a process where, as
the global becomes indeed local, steps are taken from preventing the
local to influence the shape the global takes in a specific context. The
New Age has often been described as the ultimate globalized religious phenomenon. Apologists celebrate its 'glocalization', in the
sense that national or regional forms of the New Age have emerged
in areas such as Latin America or Japan, and have in turn influenced
the global phenomenon without disrupting it. Critics claim that the
New Age is the most typical case of religious McDonaldization, and
results in a simple Americanization of previously distinctive national religious scenarios (although McDonaldization and Americanization are different phenomena: see Ritzer 1997). The problems the
New Age has encountered in the 1990s offer an excellent case study
for testing the globalization hypothesis. Does a crisis in the New Age
that is first felt in some specific countries extend to the whole world?
Do solutions to this crisis born in a specific regional context immediately extend to others?

'Next Age' is a label used in some European countries to indicate a second stage of the New Age, where utopia is abandoned and the new movement focuses on individual happiness, not global scenarios. The so-called Next Age is premised on the basis that the 'classic' New Age experienced an irreversible crisis, and something new was needed. Both ideas (namely, that the New Age was in crisis, and that a Next Age is its legitimate successor) emerged from within the movement itself, before any scholarly analysis or reconstruction. The chapter deals, first, with the crisis of the New Age, and explores a number of possible reactions to it. Secondly, it tries to describe the Next Age within the framework of the materials it uses and of similar processes in movements other than the New Age.

New Age in Crisis

A significant event spelling out the crisis of the New Age was the publication of *Reimagination of the World*, by David Spangler (possibly the most authoritative spokesperson for the New Age internationally) and William Irwin Thompson (Spangler and Thompson 1991). The book collected lectures given by Spangler and Thompson from two 1988-89 seminars at the Chinook Learning Center, an important New Age institution on Whitby Island, near Seattle. Spangler and Thompson concluded that the New Age had been 'degraded' by commercialism and was in a state of deep crisis. When the crisis of the New Age was examined by academic scholars (a paper read by J. Gordon Melton in 1994 at a seminar in Greve, Denmark, was particularly important), some of them agreed that the New Age was in a situation of crisis, but did not mention commercialism as the only (or even the most important) cause. Melton (1998) argued that, at least in the United States, there were empirically verifiable indicators of New Age's crisis, including the bankruptcy of several New Age bookstores, publishing houses, and magazines. For a number of reasons the price of crystals also fell, and far from being a mere curiosity, crystals were important commodities in the New Age economy. Melton acknowledged that commercialism was deeply resented by a number of new agers. However, he also mentioned that 'classic' New Age, a movement dating back to the 1960s in the English-speaking world, was based on the utopic, millenarian expectation of a golden age. Unlike 'catastrophic' millennialism (or premillennialism), New Age's 'progressive' millennialism (or postmillennialism: see Wessinger 1997) was optimistic. However, while catastrophic millennialism can normally claim that at least some small catastrophe has confirmed its doomsday predictions, progressive millennialism is more exposed to empirical disconfirmation. When a prophecy about an apocalyptic event fails, it is easier to claim that wars, epidemics and other catastrophic events have at any rate occurred somewhere in the world. When a millennial group announces a golden age, and fails to deliver, crisis is to be expected. Crisis, in this case, is not an automatic consequence of a millennial prophetic failure; the process only applies to progressive (rather than catastrophic) millennialism. Melton comments about a similar process in the New Age. When the announced golden age failed to materialize, New Age first resorted to messages channelled by supernatural 'entities'. It claimed that these entities should know better, and perhaps a new, golden age was appearing on Planet Earth. Human eyes were not capable of seeing it, but superhuman channelled Masters had other, safer ways of knowing. Ultimately, however — according to Melton — it could not be maintained that a new age of general happiness was in fact manifesting itself, notwithstanding any evidence to the contrary. Empirical disconfirmation prevailed on prophetic utterances. The crisis of the New Age, thus, was not a pure by-product of excessive commercialism, nor an invention of some scholars. Ultimately, the New Age went the same way as many other forms of progressive millennialism before it.

Faced with the crisis, a number of new agers simply abandoned the movement, but there is no evidence that this was the prevailing response. The two main tenets of 'classic' New Age were, firstly, that a golden age of higher consciousness was manifesting itself on Planet Earth; and secondly, that it was possible to co-operate with this happy manifestation without the need of a dogmatic creed or formal structures. The New Age was a loose network rather than a formalized structure. When crisis hit, one possible reaction was to claim that the utopic aim of the new age was still achievable, but the flexible network was not the most appropriate tool. Rather, an organized, hierarchical movement with a strong and clearly identified leadership was needed. 'Classic' New Age was not a new religious movement in the prevailing meaning of the expression. It did not recognize, and often scorned, leaders authorized by definition to declare a creed. Post-New Age movements, however, entrust precisely authoritative leaders with the task of 'saving' the New Age from its crisis. While J.Z. Knight started her career as the quintessential New Age channeller, more recently she established in Yelms (Washington) what she calls an American Gnostic school where nobody questions her right (or, rather, the right of Ramtha, the ancient spirit she channels) to define a creed and a doctrine. The New Age audience of J.Z. Knight, channeller, thus became Ramtha's School of Ancient Wisdom, a post-New Age new religious movement (Melton 1998). Older movements, marginalized in 'classic' New Age because they were closed (rather than open) structures with a precise creed and an authoritative leader, were revitalized following New Age's crisis. In Italy a number of former new agers joined Damanhur, a community of some 400 members near Turin which calls itself 'aquarian' but, at the same time, has clear creedal, statements (see Berzano 1997) and affirms the authority of the founder-leader, Oberto Airaudi, to define or change doctrine. Joining a post-New Age new religious movements is not, however, the only possible solution of the New Age crisis for those unwilling to simply abandon the movement. A larger number of new agers seem more interested in redefining New Age itself.

'Next Age'

'Next Age' is an English expression virtually unknown throughout the English-speaking New Age. It has been used mostly in Italy, and occasionally in France and other continental European countries. 'Next Age' was first used in Italy in the early 1990s to indicate a new wave of New Age music. Subsequently, the term was adopted by new agers who felt that it was necessary to distance themselves from both the excessive commercialism and failed utopias of 'classic' New Age. The term had its consecration in 1998, when the New Age Fair ('Salone del New Age') in Milan, the largest Italian New Age gathering, decided to change its name to 'New Age and Next Age Fair' ('Salone del New Age e Next Age'). The term was then adopted by nationally syndicated columnists (Barbiellini Amidei 1998), Christian counter-cult critics (Menegotto 1999), and scholars (Berzano 1999, Filoramo 1999, Introvigne and Zoccatelli 1999). Finally, it became a household name in the Italian milieu of alternative spirituality, although new agers initially argued that the label had only been adopted to protest New Age commercialism, without acknowledging that the movement in general was in a situation of crisis (for these new agers, the crisis was simply an invention of hostile anti-cultists and misguided scholars: Parodi 1998). Within the Italian New Age itself, however, others countered that the crisis had not been invented by scholars: new age utopianism had revealed itself to be a 'mirage' rather than a horizon, and something radically new was in order (Zarelli 1998, 25).

In essence, the Next Age was New Age's passage from the third to the first person. While New Age had been described as 'sacralization of the Self' (Heelas 1996), it could be argued that Next Age is rather the sacralization of myself. Classic, utopian New Age argued that Planet Earth as a whole was heading towards a new age of collective higher consciousness and happiness. Next Age recognizes that a new age may never happen collectively, in and for the whole planet. What remains possible, however, is that an enlightened minority will enter into its personal New Age through certain exercises and techniques. Whilst such techniques are not substantially different from those advocated by classic new agers, Next Age is conceived as private while New Age was public and collective. Gone is utopianism, and gone is progressive millennialism. No millennium is announced by Next Age, which confines itself to a promise of individual happiness. Whether or not individual well-being achieved by a significant number of individuals will also cause Planet Earth to heal is a vague, secondary possibility, and is no longer regarded as crucial. To this, a historical reinterpretation of the New Age is added, whereby it is claimed that the New Age was never really millenarian or utopian, that the idea of a future Aquarian Age was merely a poetic metaphor, and that individual self-transformation was always the main aim of the movement. This (quite mythological) self-reinterpretation of New Age history had already been noted by Melton in his 1994 paper (Melton 1998, 141).

Most authors and books crucial for the understanding of the Next Age date back to the 1980s and 1970s. They had remained, however, somewhat marginal in the New Age movement, precisely because they were regarded as too individualistic, potentially narcissistic, and not really interested in New Age utopias. Anthony Robbins' seminars were started in 1983 and his influential book *Unlimited Power* was published in 1987. Robbins, a former graduate of Neuro-Linguistic Programming, was however criticized in the New Age for his extreme individualism. *The Road Less Travelled*, by psychologist Morgan Scott Peck, had been published even earlier, in 1978. What is often quoted in the Next Age is the book's comment that self-sacrifice and altruism are potentially harmful to both individuals and society, while loving oneself is the key to a happy and successful life (Peck 1978, 115-16). Peck was not, strictly speaking, a new ager, and in subsequent works (including *A Different Drum*, 1987) emphasized community values and cautioned against any excessively individualistic interpretation of *The Road*. However, no subsequent book by Peck paralleled the international success of *The Road*, and many readers of the latter remain unaware of Peck's later writings and activities. In Latin countries, New Age is also greatly influenced by both the novels and the public persona of Brazilian writer Paulo Coelho, whose *O alquimista* was originally published in Brazil in 1988. Although Coelho insists that he was initiated in 1970 into a secret society, called RAM (Regnum Agnus Mundi, 'Kingdom of the Lamb of the World': see O'Connor 1998, 31) his alchemist teaches that everybody may realize his or her 'personal legend' irrespective of any society, initiation, movement, or general social perspective.

New agers who believe that we are now living in a Next Age would mention Indian medical doctor Deepak Chopra (living in the United States) as Next Age's principal spokesperson. Chopra discovered spirituality in general, and Transcendental Meditation (TM) in particular, while working as a doctor in the United States, and went on to become an important leader of American TM. He left TM in 1993, when he was already a successful author (see e.g. Chopra 1989) (with a distinctive personal voice). In 1994 he published *The Seven Spiritual Laws of Success*, and in 1995 *The Way of the Wizard*. Both books were translated into Italian in 1997, and became instant New Age best-sellers (Chopra 1997a and 1997b). Chopra does not mention a 'Next Age', but those calling themselves 'next agers' recognize in these books what they think the Next Age is all about. Although 'spiritual' laws are both universal and necessary, the immediate and possible aim is to be happy, healthy, and to live a long life (actress Demi Moore, who attended a number of Chopra's seminars, is quoted as expecting to live at least 150 years). Although the final test is that the techniques work in the readers' personal life, it is also claimed that they are very old. *The Way of the Wizard* has been particularly popular because it presents each lesson starting from an episode in the life of young King Arthur when Merlin tutored him, thus capitalizing on the growing popularity of the Grail and Arthurian cycles. Critics have noticed that young Arthur and Merlin in the book more closely resemble the corresponding characters created by Disney than the heroes of genuine medieval legends, but such criticism apparently failed to impress Chopra's fans. Chopra visited Italy in 1997, and scandalized the press by claiming that New Age is not for poor people. The latter are, he claimed, 'obsessed by money much more that the rich' and, as a consequence, incapable of spiritual growth. Only those free from material concerns are able to focus on spiritual growth and eventually enter into a new age (Benetti 1998, 31). The resulting commotion created a confrontation between 'next agers' and 'classic' new agers, and showed in a graphic way how far a spiritual teacher such as Chopra is from New Age's trademark utopia.

Next Age as Privatization

'When prophecy fails', it has been recently argued, catastrophic millennialism may still prosper through processes of cognitive dissonance (Festinger, Riecken and Schachter 1956). I would suggest that the process may indeed be different in catastrophic and progressive millennialism. When the optimistic prophecy of progressive millennialism fails, one possibility is privatization. The prophecy, it would be argued, may still come true for a selected group of individuals, although it will probably not come true for society or Planet Earth as a whole. These privatization processes have happened before: in fact, they may have happened in the aftermath of most historical forms of progressive millennialism. While it is always difficult to apply contemporary social science to events of past centuries, it could be tempting to argue that utopian early tantrism became, in late tantrism, the quest of physical immortality and other physical advantages for an elite of initiates (see White 1996). A discussion of whether this process really took place, or whether 'early tantrism' is merely a construction of Western scholars (as it has been seriously argued: see Lopez 1996) would be outside the scope of this chapter. On the other hand, it may be easier to argue that 19th century's liberal Protestantism's trust in human progress, as a way to universal happiness and peace, was progressively abandoned due to its empirical disconfirmation by a number of bloody wars. New Thought thus *privatized* the ideology of progress as something individual and unlimited (as did Christian Science also, although differently). The secular version of liberal Protestantism, 19th century's progressive modernism, experienced a similar crisis, and a *privatized* version was proposed in the form of positive thinking by Napoleon Hill (1883-1970) and (outside the English-speaking world) Émile Coué (1857-1926). After World War I had somewhat destroyed the idea of universal peace through progress, Coué could still claim that a higher state of peace may be experienced in everybody's personal, private life through positive thinking (see Centassi 1990), and similar ideas were suggested by Hill (Ritt and Landers 1995). It is of course easy to ridicule individualization processes and to claim that positive thinking is largely wishful thinking (Kaminer 1993). It is also worth noting, however, that secular positive thinking and Christian New Thought converged in one of the best-sellers of the 20th century, *The Power of Positive Thinking* (1952) by Norman Vincent Peale (1898-1993). These examples show that, when progressive millennial utopia fails, private utopias restricted to personal life may develop through privatization process. The end results are often surprisingly similar. The recipes for personal happiness of popular New Thought authors, positive thinkers, Norman Vincent Peale (and, to some extent, Morgan S. Peck) appear to be direct precursors of Chopra and other Next Age masters. It seems that the generation of a personal happiness formula through the privatization of a disconfirmed utopia may have a direct influence on the final product itself. (Tantrism is, in turn, an important presence in the milieu of those calling themselves next agers, precisely in the form of a tantrism reduced to recipes for personal and sexual happiness: see Zadra and Zadra 1997. The authors of this book manage a popular Next Age centre in Montecerignone, Italy, which promises both spiritual and sexual fulfilment).

Ultimately, the answer to the question of whether a Next Age exists depends on how the New Age is reconstructed. If one assumes, as Hanegraaff (1996) does, that utopianism was or is not crucial for New Age (or was only crucial for an earlier New Age stricto sensu), it may be argued that no crisis of the New Age ever took place and that the movement in the year 2000 and beyond is the same as in 1980s. Definitions are, of course, result-oriented tools, and no definition of the New Age is more 'true' than another. It may be argued, however, that definitions (or descriptions) of the New Age where the utopia of a forthcoming golden age was crucial were widespread within the community of the new agers, both in the English-speaking world and in some European countries, including Italy. Where utopianism was crucial, empirical disconfirmation generated a crisis (a sequel of events typical of progressive millenarianism in general). In a country such as Italy where a chain-connection existed between utopianism (or progressive millennialism) and the very expression 'New Age', the latter label was used with growing uneasiness when utopic visions had been abandoned. Hence, the emergence in Italy of the term 'Next Age' as a new designation. Whether 'Next Age' will remain an idiosyncratic Italian label, or will be adopted internationally, is ultimately not important. What is suggested in this chapter is that utopianism, well beyond the origins in the 1960s and early 1970s, continued to be crucial among an important part of the New Age community until the end of the 1980s. When utopianism was both criticized and progressively abandoned, it became increasingly common inside and outside the New Age community to conclude that the movement was experiencing a crisis (with commercialism mentioned as another factor precipitating it). At this stage, New Age (as did other forms of progressive millennialism) was subject to a process of individualization and privatization, and a 'second' New Age slowly emerged. Those emphasizing continuity may call it a new wave of the New Age. For whatever reason, discontinuity rather than continuity has been emphasized in Italy, and the label Next Age has been more widely adopted.

The fact that the crisis of the New Age extended from the United States to Europe (although not immediately) confirms that the New Age is indeed a globalized phenomenon. Contrary to some critics' claims, however, the New Age is more 'glocalized' than 'Mc-Donaldized'. Reactions to the crisis, in fact, did differ from the United States to Europe, and a country such as Italy, somewhat peripheral within the New Age's global framework, contributed with at least the label 'Next Age' — and perhaps also with a clearer perception of the crisis and its possible outcomes.

Bibliography

Barbiellini Amidei, Gaspare 1998. *New Age — Next Age*. Casale Monferrato, Alessandria: Piemme.

Benetti, Simona 1998. 'Una nuova consapevolezza'. *Ulis: Idee per la nuova era*, vol. 27 (February), 30-33.

Berzano, Luigi 1997. *Damanhur: Popolo e comunità*. Leumann, Torino: Elle Di Ci.

Berzano, Luigi 1999. *New Age*. Bologna: Il Mulino.

Centassi, René 1990. *Tous les jours, de mieux en mieux*. Paris: Robert Laffont.

Chopra, Deepak 1989. *Quantum Healing: Exploring the Frontiers of Mind/Body Medicine*. New York: Bantam Books.

Chopra, Deepak 1994. *The Seven Spiritual Laws of Success: A Practical Guide to the Fulfilment of your Dreams*. San Raphael, Calif.: Amber-Allen Publishing.

Chopra, Deepak 1995. *The Way of the Wizard: Twenty Spiritual Lessons in Creating the Life You Want*. New York: Harmony Books.

Chopra, Deepak 1997a. *Le sette leggi spirituali del successo. Vivere in armonia con la natura per realizzare se stessi* [Italian translation of *The Seven Spiritual Laws of Success*]. Milan: Armenia.

Chopra, Deepak 1997b. *L'antica saggezza dell'anima* [Italian translation of *The Way of the Wizard*]. Milan: Sperling & Kupfer.

Coelho, Paulo 1988. *O Alquimista*. Rio de Janeiro: Rocco.

Festinger, Leon, Henry W. Riecken, and Stanley Schachter 1956. *When Prophecy Fails*. Minneapolis: University of Minnesota Press.

Filoramo, Giovanni 1999. *Millenarismo e New Age: Apocalisse e religiosità alternativa*. Bari: Dedalo.

Hanegraaff, Wouter J. 1996. *New Age Religion and Western Culture: Esotericism in the Mirror of Secular Thought*. Leyden: Brill.

Heelas, Paul 1996. *The New Age Movement. The Celebration of the Self and the Sacralization of Modernity.* Cambridge, Mass.: Blackwell.

Introvigne, Massimo, and PierLuigi Zoccatelli 1999. *New Age Next Age. Una nuova religiosità dagli anni '60 a oggi.* Florence: Giunti.

Kaminer, Wendy 1993. *I'm Dysfunctional, You're Dysfunctional: The Recovery Movement and Other Self-Help Fashions.* Second edition. New York: Vintage Books.

Kurtz, Lester 1995. *Gods in the Global Village. The World's Religions in Sociological Perspective.* Thousand Oaks, Calif.: Pine Forge Press.

Lopez, Donald S. (Jr.). 1996. *Elaboration on Emptiness: Uses of the Heart Sutra.* Princeton, N.J.: Princeton University Press.

Melton, J. Gordon 1998. 'The Future of the New Age Movement'. In: Eileen Barker and Margit Warburg (eds.), *New Religions and New Religiosity.* Aarhus: Aarhus University Press, 133-49.

Melton, J. Gordon 1998. *Finding Enlightenment: Ramtha's School of Ancient Wisdom.* Hillsboro, Oreg.: Beyond Words Publishing.

Menegotto, Andrea (ed.) 1999. *New Age: 'fine' o rinnovamento? Le origini, gli sviluppi, le idee, la crisi, la 'fine' del New Age e la nascita di un nuovo fenomeno: il Next Age. Una nuova sfida per la Chiesa.* San Giuliano Milanese, Milan: Sinergie.

O'Connor, Colleen 1998. 'Magical, Mystical Quest'. *Common Boundary* 16(1) (January-February), 28-32.

Parodi, Marino 1998. 'New Age o Next Age'. *Essere: La voce della New Age* (June), 6-7.

Peale, Norman Vincent 1952. *The Power of Positive Thinking.* New York: Fawcett Books.

Peck, Morgan Scott 1978. *The Road Less Travelled: A New Psychology of Love, Traditional Values, and Spiritual Growth.* New York: Simon & Schuster.

Peck, Morgan Scott 1987. *A Different Drum: Community Making and Peace,* New York: Simon & Schuster.

Ritt, Michael J. (Jr.), and Kirk Landers 1995. *A Lifetime of Riches: The Biography of Napoleon Hill.* New York: Dutton.

Ritzer, George 1998. *The McDonaldization Thesis: Explorations and Extensions.* Beverly Hills, Calif. and London: Sage.

Robbins, Anthony 1987. *Unlimited Power.* New York: Fawcett Columbine.

Smart, Barry (ed.) 1999. *Resisting McDonaldization.* London: Sage.

Spangler, David, and William Irwin Thompson 1991. *Reimagination of the World: A Critic of the New Age, Science, and Popular Culture.* Santa Fe, N. Mex.: Bear & Company.

Wessinger, Katherine 1997. 'Millennialism With and Without the Mayhem'. In: Thomas Robbins and Susan J. Palmer (eds.), *Millennium, Messiahs, and Mayhem: Contemporary Apocalyptic Movements.* New York and London: Routledge, 47-59.

White, David Gordon 1996. *The Alchemical Body. Siddhi Traditions in Medieval India.* Chicago and London: University of Chicago Press.

Zadra, Elmar, and Michela Zadra 1997. *Tantra: La via dell'estasi sessuale.* Milan: Mondadori.

Zarelli, Edgardo 1998. 'Quale nuova era?'. *Olis: Idee per la nuova era,* vol. 28 (March), 24-25.

Part II:

Particular Cases

CHAPTER 5

Reiki: The International Spread of a New Age Healing Movement

J. Gordon Melton

Introduction

In an effort to understand the watershed changes that were occurring in social life as a result of the simultaneous advances in transportation and communications, cultural analysts and historians have appropriated *globalization* — a category set forth for the analysis of transformations in the world's economic structures in the decades since World War II. As a result of these changes, geography, especially national boundaries, has been radically reduced as a factor in the creation and sustaining of human relationships in an international and even intercontinental scale. And in the wake of these changes, there has now arisen a new global community that nurtures primary relationships and allows a level of exchange of cultural and intellectual commodities unprecedented in human history. Historically speaking, this global community consists of those people who have realized that even though as individuals we do not share the same past, we have now entered the same present.[1]

It is of some interest to explore the question of exactly when and how this global community was constituted. Was it merely the end product of a long process of global shrinking and an ever-growing

---

1. I have been particularly helped in my understanding of globalization as present history by the essays of Wolf Schäfer. See his two essays posted on the Internet, 'The Global Age' and 'What Is Contemporary History? Answer: Global History', both found at http://www.sinc.sunysb/Class/wschafer/

number of people considering themselves citizens of the world? Certainly, there is some truth in this more long-term perspective. But, of more interest is the rather sudden entrance we have made into a new era and the brevity of the transition period during which masses of people appeared to have shifted their self-image. If this shift occurred, when did it happen and what were the defining factors?

The web-like structures that facilitated the emergence of this new community has its connecting links in airport terminals, television studios, telephone offices, and the headquarters of multinational corporations. It is now undergoing rapid expansion through the Internet and the imposition of English as the world's language. The global community has become the primary instrument for the exchange and diffusion of culture. A concert in London, a speech in Nairobi, or a soccer match in Rio, can be viewed simultaneously by the people at the event and the people of the world. What is true of art, ideas, and sports, is also true of religion. We can now have a front row seat for the Pope's speeches, walk along with pilgrims in the holy land, or carry on religious discussions with people halfway around the world. The reality of the global community was vividly demonstrated on New Year Day 2000 as the events ushering in the new millennium were broadcast from and to every nation of the world.

One particularly relevant symbol of this world community is the large expatriate communities that are now found in all of the world's cities. While some of these expatriate communities are refugee communities, most are composed of immigrants who have carried their quest for advancement into the modern frontier of the global township. They are able to stay in immediate touch with their home community while enjoying all of the benefits of the new. They are able to perpetuate the culture and customs of their homeland while operating under the laws of their new domicile. The expatriate communities thus establish additional very fluid boundary lines between nations and cultures and further stimulate the swift movement of intellectual and religious ideas.

For new religions, the structures of the global community have arrived as a godsend. Each new generation has benefited from the advances in communication and transportation — Luther from the printing press, 19th century missions from the steam ship, Jehovah's Witnesses from inexpensive paper and the speed press, fundamentalism from the radio, and Pentecostalism the television. However, in the last generation, the quantum leap in our ability to communicate means that new innovative religious communities instantly have a worldwide audience. They are no longer confined to lengthy incubation periods in the community of origin or the slow laborious process of sending out disciples as missionaries. And as Falun Gong, the new Chinese qigong movement, has amply demonstrated, within a matter of a few years a new grouping can be created and become a large international religious community with little notice to the mainstream media, lost among the thousands of other spiritual communities vying for attention among the world's four billion inhabitants.

As we approach recent religious phenomena, especially the New Age movement, we then begin to ask the additional question of its relationship to globalization. Does the New Age movement, drawing as it does from both East and West, represent one of the forces pushing globalization forward or is it merely a product of said globalization, utilizing the global community for its own ends? I do not promise answers to all these questions, but they are ones to keep in mind as we explore one particular community within the New Age, the world of Reiki healers.

What is Reiki?

Reiki is a system of spiritual healing that appears to be on its way to becoming a complete religion. It emerged in the West as the New Age movement was in its initial growth phase and, like so many components of the larger movement, it has continued as the premillennialist New Age of the 1980s has been superseded by the postmillennialist emphasis upon ascension and spiritual emergence of the 1990s.

Reiki is a one of a hundred healing systems utilizing what is variously called chi, qi, prana, od, cosmic energy, or universal energy, but with a manifest uniqueness, rooted in its Chinese perspective, coming as it does out of the same thought world that produced acupuncture and qigong.[2] Reiki students learn to attune to the flow of chi

---

2. Hundreds of techniques are advocated in Chinese lore under the general label qigong to improve the flow of chi or qi. Through the 1990s, Chinese scientists have conducted numerous experiments to verify its existence and describe its nature. Cf. Wang Prisheng and Chen Guanhua, 1986; and Richard H. Lee,1999.

energy by meditating upon various symbols, and the most efficacious way to place their hands so as to stimulate the flow of chi to the client. Each level of advanced training, it is asserted, leads to a greater attunement and is accompanied by the introduction of additional symbols. Knowledge of the actual symbols are part of the confidential aspect of the Reiki system. Also, at the highest level of training, Reiki Masters learn how to teach others to do Reiki.

Reiki has some similarities to the various forms of spiritual healing that have been a part of Western religion for centuries. Although most Christian healers approach their healing work somewhat naively as simply intercessory prayer, many have been drawn to healing ministries after experiencing a sensation of the healing power and more or less privately experimenting with its activity. Spiritualists, of course, have long seen healing as a scientifically demonstrable transfer of energy, and parapsychologists have been conducting numerous experiments attempting to verify its efficacy. If one works with an energy model of spiritual healing, one assumes some need for training. One can now receive training in a variety of spiritual healing disciplines, each with its own understanding of the healing powers and differing methodologies as to the best means of manipulating them.

In the United States, healing has generally been seen as something one does for free, as an expression of one's faith. In contrast, in such places as England, Brazil, and the Philippines, Spiritualist healers have operated as professionals who work within communities that value their services. In North America, only the Christian Science and New Thought practitioners had been able to work consistently as professionals.

From the beginning Reiki practitioners were confronted with the option of becoming professional healers, with the notion that they might open an office and receive patients who would value the particular healing powers they would learn to demonstrate. While many healers claimed to tap the chi energy, the Reiki healers would be trained in special, proven, techniques granting them clearer access to the energy and would be shown the most effective way to deliver it. As a result, they should be better than the rest and achieve better results. If they chose to make Reiki their life's work, they would be deserving of pay for their professional services.[3]

3. On this professional aspect of Reiki, see William Rand, 1998.

The ability of a Reiki practitioner to operate as a professional was dependent upon the existence of clients who desired what was being offered enough to pay for it. Potential patients had to believe in the existence of chi and that the Reiki practitioners were at least among the best at evoking its healing potential. Such belief has been a building block for the Western esoteric systems at least since Mesmer, but prior to the New Age movement have been but a minuscule percentage of the population. Thus it has not been surprising to see Reiki spread simultaneously with the dramatic growth of the Western Esoteric community in the wake of the New Age movement. That movement created the public that understood and valued what a Reiki practitioner could provide.

I first encountered Reiki in the late 1970s. At the time I was pastoring a small Methodist church in Evanston, Illinois. One evening we rented the hall out to several people for what was billed as a talk on spiritual healing. As it turned out, they were hosting the first visit to the Midwestern United States of a Japanese-American teacher, Hawayo Takata (1900-1980). She turned out to be a petite elderly woman (in her late seventies) who gave a lively talk about a new healing system that she had originally learned in Japan. It was noted that she would be in the area for the next week and would be teaching the basics of Reiki. From the crowd who attended the talk, a group was assembled for the class that would teach the basic principles of doing Reiki and the subsequent intermediate class that included more advanced techniques. I did not take the classes, but several of my acquaintances did, and two of these would travel to Hawaii and take the advanced instruction that led to their initiation as Reiki Masters.

Over the last twenty years I periodically monitored the progress of Reiki. By the time Ms. Takata passed away in 1980, she had made 22 Reiki Masters and taught possibly as many as 1000 people to be Reiki healers. However, in a little more than a decade, by 1991, there were some 800 Reiki masters and more than 60,000 Reiki healers (though by no means are all, or even a majority, of these functioning as professional healers). Reiki offices and centres could be found in every major urban centre in North America and had spread through Western Europe and the countries of the former British Empire. The community has continued to expand through the 1990s. Additionally, Reiki itself has changed and diversified. A recent issue of *Kindred Spirits*, the leading UK periodical of the contemporary post-New Age spiritual emergence, for example, carried more than 20 display advertisements for various Reiki healers and healing centres. What was equally interesting was the fact that beside the notices for just simple Reiki healing there were advertisements for Ascension Reiki (ascension being a major theme of the spiritual emergence), Reiki Jin Kei Do, Annubis Reiki, Lightarian Reiki, the Tara-Mai Reiki & Seichem Teachers Association, Tibetan Reiki, and the Eternal Light Beyond Reiki. This progression from the few people Takata initiated to the present state not only of large numbers of Reiki healers, but also a plethora of variations on the original Reiki theme, paints a vivid picture of globalization in action.

The Takata Legacy

The history of Reiki really begins with Hawayo Takata.[4] She was born December 23, 1900, to a Japanese family in Hawaii. She was but 16 years old when she married Saichi Takata. She gave birth to two daughters and seemed headed for an obscure life as a housewife in the growing Hawaiian Japanese American community. Then her husband died in 1930. She secured work as a servant on a Hawaiian plantation, but was able to work her way up to become the housekeeper and then bookkeeper.

At the same time, through the early 1930s, her health deteriorated. Then in 1935 her sister died. She travelled to Japan to carry the news of the death to her parents personally and additionally use the occasion to seek out some doctors. She found her way to a surgeon, but just before she was to submit to an operation, she decided against it. Instead she asked for a referral to an alternative doctor who did not do surgery. As it happened, the brother of the surgeon was a Reiki healer. The doctor referred Takata to Chujiro Hayashi (1878-1941). Hayashi, a former navel officer had opened a clinic in which he used Reiki. After four months under Hayashi's care she was healed.

Takata was so impressed with what had happened to her that she asked Hayashi to train her as a healer. He refused; she was an Amer-

4.   The single best source on Takata's life is Helen L. Haberly, 1997.

ican. However, she was persistent, and in the spring of 1936, he relented and along with several others he gave her the basic Reiki training. The following spring she was able to take Reiki Master training from which she emerged as the 13ᵗʰ and last Master he initiated.

Shortly after becoming a Master she returned to Hawaii and opened a small clinic similar to Hayashi's in Kapaa. Hayashi visited at the beginning of 1938. His attitude toward foreigners had changed, and he named Takata as his successor (though what he intended by that designation is unclear). However, she felt empowered to continue his work and a few months later she took the opportunity to come to the mainland as the translator for a group of Buddhist ministers making a tour of the West Coast. She stayed behind to attend the National College of Drugless Physicians, a naturopathic school in Chicago.

In 1941 Hayashi died. Accounts suggest that his healing work had become incompatible with further service in the Navy. With war looming, he had been recalled to service and seemingly chose his own death instead of further involvement in killing. Back in Hawaii, Takata operated quietly through the War and post-War years during which the Hawaiian-Japanese had to bear the brunt of much anger for Pearl Harbor.

Takata operated quietly as a Reiki healer in Hawaii for several decades. It is only with her aging without a successor, coupled with the arrival of the New Age movement and the new audience for esoteric wisdom that it cultivated, that Takata decided to start teaching others as Reiki healers. More importantly, she opened those teachings to those outside of the Japanese American community. In the fall of 1973 she travelled to Puget Sound to offer her first class on Reiki to mainland students. This class launched her brief public career and introduced the public to the three-tiered Reiki system. Two years later she took the additional step and for the first time trained a new Reiki Master.

The decision to train Masters became one of her more controversial actions. She concluded that the Master status was a thing of value and that the only way to communicate its specialness to Westerners was to charge for it. She settled on a fee of U.S. $10,000. During the remaining five years of her life she would initiate 22 Masters, that is, 22 Reiki teachers who could both train new Reiki healers as well as create new Masters. Around 1977, she would visit Chicagoland, and two of the people she trained, Virginia Samdall and Ethel Lombardi, both of whom had had leadership roles in the Chicago psychic community, initially would value what they learned enough to become Masters.

Finally, in 1979, the year before she died, she would name two of the Masters as Grand Masters. One, her daughter Phyliss Furumoto resided in Hawaii. The other, Barbara Ray, lived in Atlanta, Georgia. While any of the Masters could train others, even to the point of creating new masters, there was a tendency to see Ray and Furumoto as the persons from which students should receive their Master's training.

Initially, Ray was the more assertive of the two new Grand Masters. She had received her basic Reiki Training in 1978 and in 1979 had opened a centre in Atlanta. Shortly after Takata's death she formed the American Reiki Association (after 1982 the American International Reiki Association) as a professional association for Reiki healers. In addition, she authored the first book on Takata's system, *The Reiki Factor* (1983).[5]

Phyllis Furumoto was somewhat slower to exercise her leadership as a Grand Master, but many turned to her for training and in 1983 her students founded the Reiki Alliance. Some minor differences surfaced between the two teachers, but they were minor, and could easily be seen as an attempt at product differentiation in a marketplace that became increasingly competitive. Ray trademarked the name 'Radiance Technique'. Those masters trained by Furumoto tended to designate their work as the Usui Reiki system, Usui being the name of the somewhat shadowy figure accredited with discovering Reiki. As advertisements began to appear in New Age periodicals, the word 'Radiance' or the word 'Usui' along with the Japanese letters that spelled Reiki generally identified the lineage of the Reiki healer.

Through 1980s Reiki quietly spread in Europe where it integrated with various other New Age teachings and healing practices. People were quick to see the commonalities Reiki shared with previously existing energy teachings found among New Agers. Along the path, Reiki found its way to Poona, India, and was included in the curriculum at the International Rajneesh Commune School (now Inter-

5. Barbara Ray, 1983.

national Osho Commune School). Thus it was legitimized for the already large network of disciples of Rajneesh.

Possibly the most significant change for the Reiki community came in 1989 when William Rand, a Reiki Master in the Furumoto lineage, challenged the tradition to which both Ray and Furumoto adhered, i.e., the charge of $10,000 for Reiki Master Training. Concluding that the idea was merely Takata's adaptation to the American mindset, and that the charge had become a major barrier to the further spread of the movement, he opened the Center for Reiki Training in suburban Detroit, Michigan, and began for the first time to offer not only first and second degree Reiki Training, but also Master Training for a mere $600. He also authored a textbook for the student of Reiki that included most of the Reiki heretofore confidential teachings, an important exception being the unique Reiki symbols, a key esoteric element in the technique that the Reiki practitioner acquired to gain the initial attunement to the chi energy. The establishment of the centre also challenged the widely accepted idea that a Master really should turn to Ray or Furumoto for Master training. Rand's action, in fact, stimulated the spread of the movement in the manner he envisioned. Future historians will have to judge whether his decision or the subsequent quest of Reiki practitioners to search out their roots in Japan ultimately changed the movement even more.

Reiki before Takata

Through the 1980s, little was said about the origin of Reiki. It was ascribed to a man named Mikao Usui, who had searched for and rediscovered the ancient Reiki teachings. Barbara Ray, one of the few Reiki leaders with some academic training, understood how little information about Usui had been passed on or even known by Takata. As she put it in *The Reiki Story*, 'The Story of Dr. Usui's search for knowledge would best be described as a legend. As is often true of our unfolding life process and events in the past, detailed records were not kept. The essence of Dr. Usui's story, however, is that of a person searching, as so many are today, for contact with inner truth and enlightenment.'[6]

According to the legend, Usui was a convert to Christianity. He had come to the United States, studied at the University of Chicago,

6. Ibid., 46.

and returned to Japan to teach in a seminary. Along the way, he had come to know of an ancient healing system, but did not know the particulars. His search led him to India where he discovered what he sought in a Sanskrit manuscript. The techniques he developed would be based upon a series of symbols, which, when set in motion, activate and tap universal energy. Modern people, he believed, had lost touch with this energy (or Reiki). Over the year, he established a healing centre and healed many people and reportedly initiated several Reiki masters. He wrote but little, and the tradition he initiated was passed orally from master to student. Then in the 1920s he met Dr. Chujiro Hayashi and eventually named him the next Grand Master.

This story was totally based upon Takata's memories. Few of Takata's Masters read Japanese, and they did not go to Japan to check it out. They did, however, write to the University of Chicago and to the seminary (Doshisha University in Kyoto) and discovered that no one named Usui was ever known at either school in any capacity. Many concluded that he was probably never a Christian, but most likely a Buddhist monk. The idea of his Christian background was probably suggested by Takata to assist in its acceptance in North America. However, by the end of the 1980s, the system had proved itself and had become a thriving international phenomenon. It was well integrated into the Western esoteric community, and people wanted to tie together the unanswered questions about its past.

The work of uncovering the more complete history of Reiki's origin began in 1985 when Mieko Matsui, a Japanese national who had learned Reiki from Barbara Ray, moved back to her homeland. She soon found that not only did Reiki still exist in Japan, but also that the original organization founded by Usui, the Usui Reiki Ryoko Gakkai, was alive and well. Matsui also translated Ray's book; the Japanese edition appeared in 1986. The book seemed to be the instrument for making the Japanese Reiki community aware of what had occurred because of Takata's decision to teach Reiki to the non-Japanese world. By comparing the Japanese practice with what had been passed on by Takata, Matsui first became aware of the differences between Takata's presentation of Reiki and that of the Usui Reiki Ryoko Gakkai.[7]

7. On the process of recovering the history of Reiki see the Internet site of the Traditional Japanese Reiki Foundation (http://www. japanese-reiki. org) and the Extensive Reiki Threshold site (http://www.threshold. ca/reiki/).

Matsui and other Western trained Reiki masters who would visit Japan attempted to locate and build relations with the Japanese Reiki community, but encountered repeated obstacles in their search for their roots. The Reiki leadership who held the information proved reluctant to divulge it to foreigners, even those who shared their passion for the work of Usui-sensei. Then some opening appeared in 1995 when Tashitaka Mochizuki, a Japanese Master with roots in the Japanese community as well as Western Reiki training published the first Japanese book on Reiki by a Master. More recently, another Reiki Master who developed a variant form of Reiki, Hiroshi Doi, also produced a book.

Meanwhile, in 1993 Frank Arjava Petter, a German who encountered Reiki in India at the Rajneesh Commune and later married a Japanese national, established work in Japan and advertised his willingness to train people in the Reiki Masters course. He drew a number of Japanese students, including those who had worked as Reiki healers but had never been offered the opportunity to become a Master. Over time, the diligent Petter located Usui's gravesite. More importantly, he developed relationships with several of the older members of the Reiki community. From his work, several books have appeared virtually rewriting Reiki history. In 1996, Dave King who on a visit to Japan had located a man named Tatsumi, one of the Masters who has studied with Hayashi, was left the complete set of master level notes that Tatsumi has transcribed when he completed his work with Hayashi. Thus, assembling all of these elements has enabled a more thorough history of Reiki to be created, though information about Usui remains scarce.[8]

Usui-sensei

Reiki was created by Mikao Usui (1865-1926). He was born on August 15, 1865, in Yago, Yamgata district, Gifu Prefecture. He married Sadako Suzuki with whom he had two children. He appears to have been a member of a Japanese Spiritualist group, Rei Jyutsu Kai, whose headquarters was west of Kyoto at the base of Kurama Kai, a holy mountain. He seems to have completed the study that led to his cre-

---

8. Frank Arjava Petter, 1997; and 1998.

ation of Reiki in 1914, though the actual formation of Usui Reiki Ryoho Gakkai seems to have been occasioned by a mystical experience he had while meditating on Kurama. He worked in a poorer section of Kyoto (possibly the source of his being called a Christian) and around 1921 then moved to the Harajaju section of Tokyo.

In Tokyo, he set up a school/clinic. Most students appeared to have moved into the school and worked with Usui until they had learned the system, though occasionally he travelled to other parts of the country to teach. In Shizuoka, for example, he healed Kozo Ogawa, a salesman. Ogawa would later become the leading member of the Usui organization. Also, anticipating a practice late popularized in the New Age movement, Usui is remembered as using crystals in his healing work. He appears to have taught Reiki to approximately 2000 students, several of whom opened clinics and centres around the country.

Usui wrote a brief 'Handbook' which included a description of Reiki healing (though without mentioning any of the particulars of the method), the answers to some frequently asked questions, and some poems composed by the Emperor designed to advise people on a worthy life. An English translation was included in Frank Petter's second book, *Reiki: The Legecy of Dr. Usui*.

Usui died on March 9, 1926, of a stroke. He was buried at Saihoji Temple, a traditional Buddhist temple in a Tokyo suburb. Leadership of Usui Reiki Ryoho Gakkai was passed to a Mr. Ushida. By the 1940s there were some 40 Reiki schools across Japan. In 1988, Mr. Kondo, the current president, succeeded Mrs. Koyama as head of the Usui Reiki Ryoho Gakkai.

Chujiro Hayashi appears to have been the last of Usui's students to become a Master. He was not a member of the Gakkai, but was left the title to the Usui's school/clinic in Tokyo. He operated the clinic along with two Gakkai leaders, Jazaburi Gyuda and Kanichi Taketomi (eventually the third president to the Gakkai). Hayashi had been a surgeon in the Navy, and continued his Reiki work until his death in 1942. It was through him, of course, that Reiki ultimately came to the West. His work survives through the Human and Truth Kenkysho now headed by Sanehide Aiko.

Another Usui student, Toshiiro Eguchi also created an independent lineage. Today there are no less than six Japanese Reiki lineages independent of both the Gakkai and the West (though several have absorbed elements from the West). They include the Gendai Reiki Kyokai headed by Hiroshi Doi, who has authored a book on Reiki, and Neo-Reiki. Knowledge of the vital existence of the different forms of Reiki in Japan has had significant reverberations through the international Reiki world. Most importantly, it has served to relativize the tradition as passed from Takata through Furumoto and Ray, and to lessen the ability of those who closely adhere to one of those lineages to challenge the orthodoxy of those who have created distinct Reiki schools.

The Global Scene

While Petter and others have been uncovering the history of Reiki, practitioners in the West have been making history as they have taken the Reiki dynamic and mixed and matched it with a wide variety of spiritual options now available as a result of the New Age movement. Most commonly, professionals in the New Age community added Reiki as an additional skill to offer their clients. It is quite common to go to centres at which treatments or lessons in Reiki are one possibility along with the same in meditation, psychic development, astrology, message, or additional forms of alternative healing (from aromatherapy to shiatsu). However, rather than the smorgasbord approach, several Reiki healers have attempted to integrate Reiki with another spiritual tradition/practice in such a way as to create a new variant form of Reiki that subsequently becomes one of the new Reiki traditions that are now spreading internationally.

The Tera-Mai Reiki tradition traces its beginnings to 1983 when artist Kathleen Milner took a basic Reiki course in the hope that it would add a healing quality to her artwork, but lacked the money to take the Master course. However, later in the decade she had two car accidents that had left her in a great deal of pain that did not respond to massage or physical therapy. Then, in 1989 she heard of William Rand's offering of Reiki Master classes for only $600 and decided to take the class primarily for her own benefit. The experience greatly assisted her in finally overcoming the pain.

Milner had no intention of becoming a Reiki teacher until her daughter inadvertently said something to some people that had gathered at Milner's home. Shortly thereafter she got her first request to teach Reiki and soon afterward held her first class, with four students. From that event, she launched a new career as a Reiki instructor. She taught at the 1991 Whole Life Expos in New York City and in Los Angeles. During this period she had also been doing meditation exercises with the runes and the Egyptian Cartouche, forms of divination that had been introduced into the New Age community.

Among the people to whom Milner taught Reiki was Marcy Miller, a disciple of Hindu miracle worker Sai Baba. Miller had been to a channeller in Arizona who had told her that a lady named Kathleen had already taken Reiki to a new level. Then, in India to visit Sai Baba, Miller made contact with a non-corporeal entity described only as a 'Higher Being' who told her that Takata had left out one attunement symbol and much of the initiation procedure for each of the degrees. During the 1991 Whole Life Expo at Los Angeles, Miller conveyed this information to Milner and also noted that the Higher Being had requested a meeting with the pair the following day. At that time the Higher Being revealed the missing symbol and initiation procedures. Milner began teaching this new material initially to her former students who reported that as a result of the new initiation they now felt an increase of energy. Additional information was given through Miller a short time later, and again the students reported an increase in energy.

Milner soon established her own direct contact with an array of Higher Beings like the one channelled by her friend. They told her it was time to go public with what they had taught her and would be teaching her in the future. These additional teachings, now integrated into the Reiki training, became the basis of the new Tera-Mai Reiki tradition.[9] The Tera-Mai Reiki system spread through the Reiki world, and in turn became the basis of another new variant form of Reiki developed by Milner teacher, William Rand, director of the International Center for Reiki Training in suburban Detroit. Rand used the symbols presented by Milner as a focus of meditation, as a

9. For a more complete account of Tera-Mai Reiki see Atlantis Rising, the Internet site of two Australian Reiki healers (http://www.ozemail. com.au/~teramai/).

result of which he slightly altered the uses of certain symbols as well as the attunement process. It was his experience that the energy of the entire system had shifted. He claimed that the Reiki energy had, as a whole, now became very heart centred, and he named his new approach *Karuna*, from the Sanskrit word meaning 'compassionate action'.

Rand suggested that Karuna Reiki differed from the traditional system he had received through Takata's lineage, in that in the Karuna system the energy seemed 'much more definite and focused'. This difference seemed enough to trademark the name Karuna Reiki as a means of insuring the quality of its transmission to students. Instruction consists of two separate attunements, four master symbols, and a total of eight treatment symbols. The first Karuna symbol prepares the client for a deeper healing especially as it related to reputed past reincarnations. According to Rand, it helps release karma and deeply seated issues that are often stored at the cellular level. Succeeding symbols continue the deep healing process. The second set of Karuna symbols are seen as operating at an even higher vibration, helping people connect with their higher-selves so that we may work on a deeper level leading to personal and spiritual growth.[10]

Karuna Reiki would then lead to the next variation termed 'Point of Focus'. As a young adult Ellen Louise Kahne had become interested in healing, in part to improve her own health and in part to ensure a healthy and productive life as a senior. To that end she informed herself on matters of diet and herbs, and a variety of alternative healing methods from chiropractic to yoga. She began her Reiki training with Josephine Miranda, a Master in the Furumoto tradition. After working with her for more than two years, she attended William Rand's school and completed her Master training and the additional Karuna training. Kahne considered herself an intuitive person, and learning the Karuna variation of Reiki merely legitimized her search for insights from all the different Reiki variations and the further development of Reiki by herself. According to Kahne,

10. Karuna healing is discussed on William Rand's Internet site for his International School of Reiki Healing (http://www.reiki.org).

Point of Focus techniques use intensified, focused, and grounded Reiki healing skills (...). A focused energy matrix (vibration field) is induced as the first step in healing. This preparation and other Point of Focus healing techniques deepen and accelerate Reiki healing (...) as well as enhancing all other healing skills and disciplines (including massage, physical and occupational therapies, nursing, psychological counseling and all allopathic and alternative medicine modalities).

Among the most interesting developments at the edge of the Reiki community is the Star Esseenia Temple of Ascension Mastery. Reiki healer August Starr had an intense psychic experience during a solar eclipse in 1991. She described it as having her own higher self 'walk-in' and take over her body. As part of the experience, she was told to abandon the Reiki healing that she had been practicing and to prepare for a new set of fifth dimension energies that she would channel for the coming ascension of the race. Subsequently, she has discovered a set of new higher healing energies, to which she now offers attunement.

August Starr has placed her new healing work in the context of the larger post-New Age ascension teachings concerning the transformation of some humans into 'fifth dimension' beings in general, and has further adopted the particular teachings of a New Age channel named Solara. Solara had suggested that beginning in the 1990s and continuing through 2011, many people would experience ascension, an intense inner alteration. The symbol under which this transition would occur was '11:11'. August Starr suggested that the '11:11' symbol triggers a successive set of issues which those treading the ascension pathway must deal with and lay to rest.

For each set of issues, Starr is developing a set of healing modalities with which to confront them. At the same time, as new healing energies are made available to her she has been training what are termed Star Teams to attune to those energies and utilize them for themselves and others. Starr, also a channel of the space brothers of the Ashtar Space Command, has placed her new healing work within the context of her channelled messages from the extraterrestrial Higher Beings.

The Traditionalist Reaction

In stark contrast to the evolving systems of Milner, Rand, Kahne, and Starr, the concurrent recovery of the history of Reiki led another group of practitioners to search for the original system of healing as taught by Usui. In 1996, Melissa Riggail made contact with one of Chujiro Hayashi's students named Tatsumi. Tatsumi had notes that had been passed from Usui through Hayashi, and he made these available to Riggail. Thus, utilizing the material from Tatsumi and the other discoveries of the mid 1990s, Riggail created the Traditional Japanese Reiki Foundation.[11] The leaders of the Foundation understand Usui as someone who brought together elements of traditional Oriental teachings, especially Tendai Buddhism, Taoist qigong (that has enjoyed considerable publicity in the West in the last year due to the Chinese government's conflict with Falun Gong, a qigong group that emerged in strength in the 1990s), and traditional Chinese medicine.

Chinese medicine postulates the existence of a set of energy meridians running through the body. The impairment of health suggests that the free flow of energy through these meridians is inhibited. The stimulation of energy flow is, for example, the purpose of acupuncture, and the placement of the acupuncture needles at points along the meridians is designed to remove any obstacles to that flow. In Reiki, the student is taught to interact with the client's energy system and the hand placements are also related to stimulating the downward flow of energy in the body, especially along what is termed the gall bladder meridian which runs vertically from the head to the toe.

Also, it had been discovered that Usui used a slightly different set of symbols from those passed on to her students by Takata. They were derived from a Buddhist ritual and consisted of three symbols representing Power, Love and Light coupled with a fourth symbol that serves to empower the other three.

Usui taught a set of affirmations that were to become common to the different Reiki systems:

---

11. See the Foundation's Internet site (http://www.japanese-reiki.org).

The Secret Method of Inviting Blessings
The Spiritual Medicine of Many Illnesses

For today only; anger not, worry not.
Do your work with appreciation.
Be kind to all people.

In the morning and at night, with hands held in prayer,
think this in your mind, chant this with your mouth.
The Usui Reiki method to change your mind and body for the
better.

It appears that although Usui did not publish material on Reiki, he
had a notebook manual that new Masters copied, and from which
they taught. A copy of the original 'Handbook' in Usui's handwriting
was found in 1997 and published by Frank Petter in his book, *Reiki:
The Legacy of Dr. Usui*. In the 'Handbook', Usui answers a number of
questions on Reiki and reproduces a selection of poetry written by
the Meiji Emperor as advice on a worthy life. That manual is now
used as a textbook by the traditionalists.

The new traditionalists have specifically criticized the mixing of
Reiki with Tibetan teaching. They see the Indo-Tibetan understanding of the body, built around the set of energy vortexes known as
chakras, as incompatible with the understanding of the body's energy
system as understood in traditional Chinese medicine. They also
argue that this injection of Tibetan teaching is based upon the false assumption that Usui went to Tibet to study.

Traditionalists' comments on Tibetan traditions are specifically directed at Reiki Jin Kei Do, which asserts credentials reaching back to
the original teachings of Usui as passed through Hayashi to a Zen
monk named Takeuchi. Reiki Jin Kei Do sees itself as a more meditative approach to Reiki. The raising of the healing energies, it claims,
leads to an elevation of consciousness. Physical healing is a mere by-
product of that new consciousness. Sensei Takeuchi passed the Reiki
empowerments and meditations originally received from Mikao
Usui to Seiji Takamori (b. 1907). Takamori, in turn, became interested
in tracing the 'true' origins of Reiki that he felt lay in Tibet. For 20
years he searched through India, Nepal, and Tibet, and eventually

located monks who practiced the 'Buddho System of Healing', described as a method similar to but more complete than Reiki. After years of study, Takamori received all the secret teachings and energy transmissions, and returned to teach what he now called EnerSense. In 1990, he taught Ranga Premaratna the four stages of EnerSense along with the teachings and empowerments of Reiki. It was Premaratna who named the teaching Reiki Jin Kei Do- Reiki or the Way of Compassion and Wisdom. The Tibetan Reiki system has now spread worldwide.[12]

Reiki as a Global Movement

The several forms of Reiki briefly summarized above are by no means all of the variations of the system released upon the world by Ms. Takata in the 1970s, nor even the most exotic of those variations.[13] Surfing the Internet can quickly reveal scores of new Reiki systems. What has been most fascinating about Reiki has been the contrast of its growth through its first two generations (when after several decades of being confined to Japan it was quietly transferred to Hawaii), as opposed the last two decades (i.e., its sudden transfer into a non-Japanese setting and global spread climaxed by its return to its point of origin). Once brought back to its homeland, it has stimulated and revived the original Reiki community.

Even after Reiki was introduced on the American mainland, it spread relatively slowly until the end of the 1980s when William Rand dropped the prices for third level training. By this time, Reiki had been introduced into the New Age movement that included several million adherents in the United States alone. Thus, once Rand began training Reiki masters in mass, the New Age supplied a ready-made community of believers who already accepted the basic teaching upon which Reiki was built and hence a network from which an initial clientele could be recruited. Additionally, the New Age network provided multiple lines of contact by which the Reiki teachings

12. Information on Reiki Jin Kei Do can be found at its many websites such as: http://world.std.com/-pwarren/ or http://www.healingtouch.co.uk/ pa-j-int.htm
13. For example, see Karyn K. Mitchell, 1998.

could be transferred to other English-speaking countries and to continental Europe.

The global New Age community emerged in the 1970s as long-standing ties among Theosophists and various esotericists expanded and mingled with new international networks established by followers of various Eastern teachers. The rapid spread of this network was made possible by the prior development of the global communications/transportation web mentioned above. It both utilizes the technological web while pushing forward the cultural and social processes that are still transforming our spatial consciousness. Those brought into Reiki have been immediately made part of an international community. At the same time, as Reiki spread, individual teachers from different parts of the world felt empowered to change the system and introduce that change back into the network in such a way that it impacted the entire Reiki world.

This brief look at Reiki merely offers a brief probe of the complex multifaceted reality of globalization. Reiki is one of a host of recent movements that came into view in the 1970s, simultaneously with the emergence of the global technological web, and have been able to actualize the potential inherent in the web's existence. At the same time it has come into existence as a self-conscious community of people who understand their participation in the global awareness of our common present. It is hard to think of a movement birthed in the 1950s or 1960s that spread so rapidly, though, of course, many have now attuned themselves to the new technological possibilities.[14]

Bibliography

Haberly, Helen L. 1997. *Reiki: Hawayo Takata's Story.* Olney, Md.: Archedigm Publications.
Lee, Richard H. 1999. *Scientific Investigation into Chinese Qigong.* San Clemente, Calif.: China Healthways Institute.

---

14. The decentralized movement built around the channelled material known as *A Course in Miracles,* originally published in 1975, appears at first glance to have followed a similar rapid global expansion as has Reiki.

Mitchell, Karyn K. 1998. *Reiki Mystery School*. Oregon, Ill.: Mind River Publications.

Petter, Frank Arjava 1997. *Reiki Fire*. Twin Lakes, Wisc.: Lotus Light Publications.

Petter, Frank Arjava 1998. *Reiki: The Legacy of Dr. Usui*. Twin Lakes, Wisc.: Lotus Light Publications.

Rand, William 1998. *Reiki for a New Millennium*. Southfield, Mich.: Vision Publications.

Ray, Barbara 1983. *The Reiki Factor*. New York: Exposition Press.

Wang Prisheng and Chen Guanhua 1986. *Relax and Calming Qigong*. Hong Kong: Peace Book Co.

CHAPTER 6

Homo accumulans and the Spiritualization of Money

Lisbeth Mikaelsson

> *Go first class all the way and the universe will respond by giving you the best* [1]

Prosperity Literature and the Globalization Process

Surfacing in books from the 1980s and 1990s, how to get rich and be successful in life is the key question in a present New Age trend. Being preached by leading New Age figures in the last decade, the gospel of affluence is ensured to have a global audience. Such prosperity discourse represents a mythologizing of money and riches, framed in the spiritual empowerment of the individual. My intention is to discuss some dimensions of globalization which are related to the gospel of affluence in its literary manifestations, globalization here being understood as a multi-dimensional process.[2]

My first topic concerns the literary system, which contributes to make New Age a global religious movement. New Age is a literary culture. Books are one of the main vehicles for spreading New Age ideas, easy to get and even reaching audiences not in other ways concerned with alternative matters. In discussing globalization in relation to New Age, the spread of literature around the world can hardly be ignored. This literature is to a great extent produced in the English language, a fact that does not prevent its being sold and read in Scandinavia for instance, where most people have a good command

1. Chopra 1993, 28.
2. Cf. Tomlinson 1999; Beck 2000.

of English. The considerable diffusion of New Age literature in Norway, which will be my point of reference in this article, is a sign of participation in an international literary market, as well as an indication of the presence of New Age ideas in Norwegian culture. Prosperity manuals are no exception. All the volumes referred to are on sale in Norwegian bookstores, thus exemplifying literary 'glocalization', or, some local ramifications of the international literary system.[3] Questions to be raised in this particular case relate to the local impact of foreign authors, books and ideas, and how far native voices and agendas are manifesting themselves.

Secondly, I will try to argue that prosperity discourse, as it is met in this literature, reflects a kind of global or globalizing view of reality in Western culture, which is an important aspect of the globalization process. I do not refer to a definite worldview, but to a variety of conceptions and pragmatic attitudes, which represent the world as a huge, exploitable accumulation of resources and an aggregate of systems where basic elements are constantly flowing. Persons, goods, money, ideas, images — a world of economy, information, science, and travel, or in psychological terms, a world of prosperity, indulgence, change, choice and possibilities. New Age money talk is here understood to be part of a cultural world-construction, its language and ideas being packed with individualism, consumerism,[4] and the marketing discourse typical of the capitalist system.[5]

Three aspects of the world construction inherent in spiritual prosperity manuals will be assessed here:

a) the legitimating of consumption and desire on the level the individual or, in other words, the nature of the individual who is fit to live in the global world of multiple possibilities;

3. Cf. Robertson 1995. The concept of glocalization counters the idea that globalization neccessarily means homogenization.
4. Consumerism is understood as a way of life dominated by consumption. Cf. Miles 1998, 4. The amalgam of structures and practices distinguishing consumerism is increasingly becoming global in scope as well as pervading our everyday lives in Western societies.
5. Paul Heelas has formerly pointed out connections between New Age and today's capitalism. Heelas 1992; 1993; 1996.

b) the cosmic vision of abundance; and
c) how money becomes a cosmic-personal symbol for a global, post-industrial world.

The Literary Market

New Age is a market in both a metaphorical and an economic sense. This is clearly demonstrated by the literary system. New Age literature includes a range of topics and agendas offered to the public through general bookstores and book clubs, as well as specialized New Age shops, a literary system securing a broad impact of New Age ideas. 'Hard core' new agers as well as ordinary people can easily find an assortment of New Age books, some of them international bestsellers, like James Redfield's *The Celestine Prophecy* or Deepak Chopra's *The Seven Spiritual Laws of Success*. Books are an important specimen of New Age goods, easily crossing national borders as well as barriers between hard core and mainstream. Large editions bring fortunes to their authors while making them public gurus with international reputation.

The literary system consisting of publishers, shops, books, authors and customers/readers is an effective distributor of religious ideas. The literary market is providing myths and symbols for individual identity construction, alternative worldviews and cures, all well adapted to the dynamics of supply and demand characteristic of liberal, postmodern culture. Western religious gurus are increasingly authors staging the prophet role, and in some cases international networks of supportive readers are organized. The success of the prosperity manuals on the market is an indication of their having some positive resonance among people. The import of the 'be rich and successful' theme in a country like Norway may forebode significant changes in religious and ethical orientation.

Compared to other literary New Age topics like astrology or health, the volumes about economic success are few in number. If this conflation of spiritual and consumerist values is not yet dominant within the New Age, it corresponds with the main thrust of New Age development towards becoming a market of practitioners offering a range of articles and treatments to individual customers. The prosperity gospel can be said to represent a summit in this adaptation to the capitalist, consumerist society.

The majority of New Age books seem to be produced in USA, it is therefore also a question of the spread of American-styled ideas and values through the literary system. This is particularly true of the prosperity discourse, which is basically a packet of ideas reaching back to American positive thinking in the nineteenth century. However, what is meant by 'American' in this context is not clear. American New Age is a melting pot, mingling ideas extracted from different religious traditions and parts of the world. American New Age books may not be very different from British, Danish, or Norwegian counterparts. However, USA represents a huge audience and big money, large publishing companies and a vital new religious environment, which cooperate in bringing American books and their authors to the forefront. More than most other New Age topics, the 'rich and successful' theme is infused with values that have a long history in American culture.[6]

Deepak Chopra is probably the best illustration of a multicultural New Age biography as well as an American author in the 1990s with a global impact. Chopra, a prolific writer in alternative health and spiritual development, is of Indian descent and has a religious background in Transcendental Meditation. Several of his books have been international bestsellers, including the above-mentioned *The Seven Spiritual Laws of Success*, which appeared in 1994. By 1997 Chopra had sold 10 million books in 30 languages.[7] Chopra's enthusiastic readers have joined The Global Network of Spiritual Success, a worldwide union where members systematically study his spiritual laws and report their effects. The author gives lectures and seminars around the world, in 1997 charging, according to *Newsweek*, U.S. $25,000 for a single lecture. CDs, herbal products, seasonings and massage oils are also produced by Chopra's enterprises.[8] No wonder the *Newsweek* entry called him 'the local healer of the global village'.[9]

6. Cf. Glickman 1999; Wilde 1998, xii-xiii.
7. Leland and Power 1997, 46.
8. Leland and Power 1997, 47, 50.
9. Power 1997, 51.

As a hedonistic trend, the gospel of affluence differs from the ascetic Calvinism that Max Weber maintained could explain the rise of capitalism. It is no matter of course that such ideas should gain much ground in Scandinavia. Like Sweden and Denmark, Norway is religiously rooted in the Lutheran branch of Protestantism and its welfare state is based on social values of equality and solidarity. This social model has had a broad acceptance and is still supported by all the main, political parties. However, Norway is also a rich, modern society, very much oriented towards USA. Materialism, individualism and privatization are gaining ground in society at large.

Judging by his presence on the literary market, Deepak Chopra's charisma and gospel of infinite possibilities has found some response in Norway. One proof is Tanum, a centrally situated bookstore in Oslo with the largest department of alternative literature in Northern Europe. Tanum has included eleven works by Chopra in their 1999 catalogue, six of them translated into Norwegian. In the field of money and success Chopra has published two booklets called *Creating Affluence* (1993) and the above-mentioned *The Seven Spiritual Laws of Success* (1994).[10] While *Creating Affluence* has not sold particularly well on the Norwegian market, the Norwegian edition of *The Seven Spiritual Laws of Success* has become a bestseller.

Self-help books about getting rich constitute a minor element in Tanum's large alternative stock. The fact that no Norwegian authors have contributed to the genre is also a sign that this spiritual call has not yet gained a firm footing in the country. The only volume originally published in Norwegian is the booklet *Formelen til suksess*[11] (1987) by American military psychologist James Holiman. He has lived and worked in Norway for many years, and is an author of spiritual literature. Other spiritual prosperity authors represented on the Norwegian scene include Stuart Wilde, lecturer and best-selling author in the human-potential movement, who has published at least three volumes about abundance, the volume available in Norway in 1999 is *The Money Bible* from 1998.[12] The prosperity and success theme

10. In Norwegian the book is called *Suksessens sju åndslover*. It was published in 1996.
11. The title could be translated 'The success formula'.
12. The other two are: *The Trick to Money Is Having Some* and *Life Was Never Meant to Be a Struggle*, cf. Wilde 1998, vii.

is however integrated in many New Age writers' ideas of spiritual self-development. Therefore, its diffusion is much broader than the books particularly focused on money. One example is *Real Magic* (1992), a book written by America's leading love-yourself philosopher, Wayne Dyer.[13] Also available in Norway is Sanaya Roman and Duane Packer's volume *Creating Money* (1988), which is fully focused on having money and is also a definite New Age production in its insistence on being channelled by two spiritual masters, Orin and Da-Ben. Roman and Packer publish messages from these personages in several books.[14]

In spite of this literary supply, prosperity and success are not considered by native booksellers and publishers to be mainstream New Age topics in the Norwegian context.[15] Also, the large, yearly exhibitions by alternative practitioners ('Alternativmessen') are certainly staging New Age as a market, but the 'be rich and successful' agenda is hardly noticeable in this setting. Judging from these exhibitions, health, divination and spiritual self-development (without the prosperity ingredient) are the main themes among Norwegian new agers. The leading New Age magazine in Norway, *Nettverk-Nytt*, has ignored the topics of prosperity and success. A 1999-interview with Deepak Chopra by the editor has a critical note, confronting Chopra with his seeming lack of social and ecological conscience.[16] Partly due

13. A Norwegian translation, *Ditt magiske liv*, appeared in 1996.
14. Cf. Hanegraaff 1996, 41, 56f.
15. Grouped with other alternative editions in Norwegian book-selling contexts, some of the texts in the money and success genre cannot be reckoned as New Age. American journalist Napoleon Hill (1883-1979) is one of the pioneers of the genre, and his *Think and Grow Rich Action Pack* has had seven million readers since its first publication, according to the 1998 Danish edition of the book, *Tænk dig rig!* Hill's message is based on his interviews before the Second World War with 504 very rich Americans, who taught him a success formula that could work for ordinary people. Unity Church minister Catherine Ponder is the best-selling author of 'The Millionaires of the Bible' series. Her book *The Dynamic Laws of Prosperity* from 1962 came forth in a ninth printing in 1997 and is found in Tanum's stock. Jerry Gillies' *Moneylove*, originally published in 1978, has a purely materialistic perspective. A Norwegian translation of *Moneylove* appeared in 1993, *Pengeglede*.
16. Solum 1999.

to the considerable influence of Anthroposophy, nature romanticism and anti-materialism have been important ingredients in Norwegian culture, not least in alternative circles.[17] This circumstance may explain why the gospel of affluence has, so far, no public advocates among prominent Norwegian new agers or alternative people.

It should be mentioned, however, that present-day Norwegian culture is as influenced by consumerism as the rest of Europe. Oil economy has transformed the country from being relatively poor to becoming one of the richest societies in our part of the world. The Christian charismatic movement and New Age are increasingly undermining the spiritual hegemony of the Lutheran state church. Looking only in expert New Age circles for the impact of the affluence gospel can justly be criticized, in that the possible influence of such literature on the general public is not taken into consideration. Interestingly, people belonging to the charismatic movement in Norway are listening to American financial prophets preaching a 'biblical economy' or a Christian gospel of economic growth and success, which can be compared with the New Age variety.[18]

The similarity between the New Age and other psycho-spiritual 'be rich and successful' books is a sign that New Age authors have learnt from their predecessors, and also that their books, like the others, are written for many kinds of prosperity-seekers, not primarily alternative people. A related type of literature is the sort called 'behavioural finance' or 'behavioural economics', which is an area bordering on psychology on the one hand and finance on the other, some directed at professional practitioners in the stock market, others at ordinary people.[19]

The Legitimating of Consumption and Desire

Characteristic of the prosperity and success manuals are the oracular, authorial voice, professing insight into the secrets of life. The author speaks with convincing authority on his subject, but more in the style of a commercial on television than a reflective philosopher, in spite of

17. Cf. Waage and Schiøtz 2000.
18. Cf. Haaland 1998, Reigstad 1995.
19. Cf. Orman 1997; Belsky and Gilovich 1999; Shefrin 2000.

the rather complicated ideas embodied in, for instance, Chopra's discourse. The scientific rhetoric manifested in terms like 'laws of nature' and 'universal laws' for rather elementary maxims are ingredients in such authority construction. At the same time the author relates to the reader as an adviser, a kind of benevolent magician and spiritual master, willing to share his brilliant techniques, while reminding the reader with pressing urgency that she/he is a spiritual being made for success and prosperity.

All the above-mentioned authors recommend the desire for prosperity as morally and spiritually legitimate. They insist that life is full of possibilities for becoming rich, and that people deserve to have a high material standard. The last point, that everyone deserves to prosper, is repeated again and again as a suggestive mantra. None of the authors voice objections against using manifestation techniques like affirmation and visualization to obtain money or material items.

The implied reader is not supposed to have any specialist knowledge of economy. In fact, economy in the ordinary sense is hardly what the books are about. Rather it is the individual person's psychological attitude to money and abundance, which is put in the context of meditation, manifestation, self-development and positive thinking. The books by Chopra, Holiman, Roman and Packer are even presented as magical tools for the readers' use.

Chopra's most specific advice to the prosperity-seeker is that he should read Chopra's own book, *Creating Affluence* in a systematic fashion. The whole book should be perused once, and after that a dose of five pages a day should be made a reading habit. Affluence of all kinds will then follow automatically.[20] Becoming rich does not even depend on making a decision to be rich. Chopra explains such magical effects with mental awareness. From awareness comes the ruling and organizing power on all levels of existence, and this power operates in our lives independently of our knowledge of it. If Chopra's wealth consciousness shapes one's awareness of money and riches through reading, personal reality will be organized in a way that automatically creates affluence. Holiman also places a similar accent on the effects of awareness, and in addition, belief.

Roman and Packer recommend a type of divination, which has its

20. 1993, 13.

parallel in bibliomancy. That means the book should be opened at random and the first paragraph one's eyes meet should be seen as a message directed particularly to oneself about a specific question. The Christians who practise this kind of divination believe that God himself is answering through the words in the Bible. Roman and Packer will have it that the reader's higher self gives a helpful sign or a message through their book.[21]

Visualizations and affirmations (verbal messages directed to one-self) are among the other methods suggested by these authors. Both are used in the New Age to cure sickness, improve one's relations to other people or develop spiritually. Stuart Wilde recommends the reader to:

Start by reminding yourself that there's loads and loads of money around. Perhaps it sounds a bit silly, but you ought to begin every day by telling yourself that there is no shortage of money. In fact, there are untold trillions of dollars, yen, pounds, D-marks, and so on swishing about — more than you could ever spend.[22]

Proposed techniques also include rituals,[23] or the reading of biographies of successful people.[24]

The individual who wants to be rich or have success is told to accept his/her desire, improve his/her self-image, trust his/her intuition, invest in his/her own development and have confidence in the world. This is general advice to the prosperity-seeker. None of the authors seem to have much trust in hard work. Dyer recommends people to establish a 'miracle fund' as a gift to oneself, because, as he says, it is important to give oneself rewards.[25] Chopra is generally moving on the higher, cosmic levels. As economic adviser he is about as specific as Maharishi Mahesh Yogi was when TM was planning a world peace project. 'Where is all the money going to come from?'

21. 1988, xxi.
22. Wilde 1998, 2.
23. Wilde 1998, 9.
24. Holiman 1987, 93.
25. Dyer 1996, 211.

somebody asked. 'From wherever it is at the moment', replied Maharishi.[26] Chopra cites the incident as a model of the kind of mentality the prosperity-seeker should develop.

The methods for changing consciousness are repeatedly characterized as magical by the authors themselves. In this case the magic is based on elementary psychological knowledge about the constitution of human consciousness and phenomena like autosuggestion.[27] Magic becomes equivalent to manipulation of consciousness. The idea of the unconscious is a general condition for this way of thinking. Without going into details about the authors' conceptions of the unconscious, three ideas seem to be especially relevant. Firstly, people are influenced by ideas and structures in their unconscious without realizing it. Secondly, the unconscious can be manipulated, or 'reprogrammed'. Thirdly, the unconscious does not know the difference between what is true and false. The assumption is that one can feed the unconscious with fictive 'information', and if it is done with strength and conviction, the unconscious will start to believe it. If you are poor, you may convince your unconscious that you are rich by consistently affirming or visualizing money. Your brain will then tell your body that you are rich. Consequently you will behave like a rich person. The change in yourself will make other people respond differently to you. Mental efforts like attention, belief, and manifestation techniques will therefore start a favourable spiral. Similar ideas lie behind mass media advertising, and parallel lines can be drawn concerning its rhetoric. One may ask if the quasi-religious language of so much present advertising, abounding in 'energies', 'magic' and 'miracles', is paving the way for belief in the mystical effects of affirmations, visualizations and the like.

The psychological manner of reasoning shines through also when it comes to the concept of abundance. The authors do not specify the quantities needed for somebody to be considered affluent. If you feel rich, you are rich. Affluence is seen as a combination of material and psychological states. When our needs and desires are gratified spontaneously and without much effort, we experience affluence.

A connecting line is drawn between money and personality,

26. Chopra 1993, 56.
27. Cf. Holiman 1987, 92.

makng money a personality symbol. Money becomes a prolongation of the personality, or a mirror, which tells stories of who we are.[28] A narrow, limited personality neither attracts money nor is able to handle riches. In Wilde's poignant words: 'Big heart = big money. Little heart = little money'.[29] Prosperity becomes the sign of a healthy emotional life. The truly affluent person loves himself, believes in himself, has faith in his success, and confidence that his good fortune is deserved. Joy, health, happiness, and vitality are ingredients in affluence according to Chopra.[30] The concept 'wealth consciousness' covers all these personality traits, which are more decisive than one's financial situation when it comes to affluence. A person with wealth consciousness does not trouble himself about the lack of money. Neither do other worries destroy his peace of mind. Easy-going wealth consciousness is a condition of affluence in the New Age sense, as well as an aspect of it.

Wealth consciousness explains why some people have success in their lives and, correspondingly, poverty consciousness is the reason why people fail or stay poor. Psychologically it has to do with the belief already mentioned, that attention stimulates growth.[31] Wilde explicitly refuses to view lack of money as misfortune, bad luck or bad karma, insisting that it results from psycho-spiritual error.[32]

The affluent, spiritually enlightened person is described by Holiman as the eschatological new being, released from limitative religious beliefs and childish conceptions, a true citizen of the new age, self-confident, balanced and successful.[33]

The Cosmic Vision of Abundance

In cosmological terms people's riches are part of the endless prosperity of the endless universe. In the naturalizing language of Chopra, affluence is reality, having the same origin as 'a cluster of nebulas, a

28. Wilde 1998, 8.
29. 1998, 27.
30. 1993, 17.
31. Chopra 1993; Gillies 1993, 11; Wilde 1998, 11.
32. 1998, xiv.
33. 1987, 32f.

galaxy of stars, a rain forest, or a human body...'. Even thoughts have the same source. This common, universal source of all forms of existence is the reason why humans can fulfil every desire they have.[34] The cosmological vision of abundance is expressed in a language taking key concepts from physics, thereby adding to the scientific ring of the rhetoric. Both Wilde and Chopra explicitly refer to quantum theory in their works. Wilde maintains that his metaphysics of money follows the same path as the laws of quantum physics. To have money entails transformation from a hazy-wave state of ideas (dreaming of money, wishing for money etc.), into a solid state in the shape of a coin, a bank note, or a positive bank balance.[35] Chopra sees the individual's wealth consciousness as a deeper connecting link with the innermost, spiritual core of the universe. Referring to the world conception in quantum physics, this core is described as an immaterial, unified field of energy, thought, and information. According to Chopra's version of quantum physics, material existence, as we perceive it is an illusion, because the innermost essence of the universe has proved to be 'thinking non-stuff'. Not verbal thoughts, but preliminary thoughts in the shape of intentions. Before thoughts become verbal, they are intentions.[36] At the same time thoughts are energy, and energy is thus thought. The unified field comprising thought/information and energy is the foundation of the world and the source of all types of existence. It is characterized as pure attention, or pure consciousness.[37] As 'the field of all possibilities' it has inexhaustible power and creativity. It is made equivalent with the cosmic self, and Chopra does not hesitate to call it 'God'[38] or 'Brahman'.[39] Humans can have experiential knowledge of the field. This particularly happens through meditation, when one knows without the use of words. Meditation therefore brings experience of pure being.[40]

34. Chopra 1993, 17f.
35. 1998, 5.
36. 1993, 20f.
37. 1993, 66.
38. 1993, 33.
39. 1993, 73.
40. 1993, 67. Cf. Holiman 1998, 80.

In this way our human thinking becomes an integral part of the flows of information and energy on the cosmic scale. That is why people's thoughts decide what kind of worlds they live in. Consequently poverty thoughts are responsible for poor life situations. Implied in Chopra's philosophy is the conclusion that poverty thoughts also represent a false understanding of existence. Since the universe is infinite in affluence and possibilities, individuals with wealth consciousness have a more adequate understanding of life. They are in fact more enlightened. The Puritan capitalists interpreted their economic success as a sign of their salvation. Chopra's philosophy makes material affluence a sign of the connection between the individual and the cosmic self. Perhaps one could say it is the consumer version of Atman's integration with Brahman.

The authors unanimously make money into a holistic symbol, uniting individual and world, higher and lower self, consciousness and material existence, body and mind. The concept of *energy*, with its physical as well as occult meanings, is the vehicle linking cosmos, consciousness, and money in a dynamic manner. Money is a symbol of the life energy we use and exchange in our dealings with the universe, as Chopra would say. The body becomes an instrument to administer energy.[41] According to Wilde money is a solidified form of energy, subject to universal laws. To be ready for abundance means one has to be in tune with the flow of energy that money represents. You have to become 'the embodiment of energy in motion — that is flexible, fluid, and fast on your feet'.[42] Or as Orin and DaBen characterize the laws of money from their spiritual perspective:

Money is energy, and energy exists in all realms. The spiritual laws of money are universal energy laws that create abundance: the principles of ebb and flow, unlimited thinking, giving and receiving, appreciation, honoring your worth, clear agreements, magnetism, and more.[43]

41. Chopra 1996, 34, 57.
42. 1998, 14.
43. Roman and Packer 1988, xxvi. Cf. Chopra 1993, 48, 52.

Both energy holism and the hyperbole rhetoric suggesting infinite possibilities and unlimited wealth can be understood as globalizing discourse. The authors' speech demonstrates how money has become the one necessary prerequisite for gratifying desires in our society. Their magic formulas for obtaining affluence point to advertising rhetoric as well as the spiritual universe of New Age. Chopra's obviously Indian-inspired philosophy of the world as a big dream machine, which 'churns out dreams and turns them into reality',[44] becomes a cosmological assurance that 'every dream you have will come true'. If this type of reality construction is gaining ground, one reason can be sought in the fact that the relationship between production and economy is becoming more and more blurred, due to different features characteristic of late capitalist society and our increasingly global world, as I will try to argue below.

Money: A Cosmic-personal Symbol for a Global, Post-industrial World

In his book *Dimensions of the Sacred* (1996) Ninian Smart rightly maintains that religions have economic dimensions, which are generally overlooked by religious scholars. He makes an important point about the transition from farming and fishing societies to industrial societies and some of the consequences of this transition on the mythical level. In pre-industrial society people conceive economic realities in cosmological terms. Gods give the necessary rain and sunshine for crops to grow, they supply the fish in the sea or the game to hunt. In industrial society human beings realize that they themselves are the economic actors. Men build industries, make technological inventions, create work for their fellow human beings and establish social institutions. In such societies social and economic power is ascribed to people and social structures. Men acknowledge their dependence on each other, while the economic aspects of the gods perish.[45]

I think it is relevant to draw this line of thought further, to our present situation, which is often characterized as the post-industrial

44. 1993, 93.
45. Smart 1996, 268.

society. What is new today is the complexity and opacity of late capitalist culture with its global ramifications. Multi-national companies,
the world of international finance and its operations, currency speculations and stock exchange — many factors in our present situation
cooperate to make economy an impenetrable mystery for people in
general. Some fairy-tale personalities become immensely rich because they have the intuition and boldness to do the right financial
manoeuvres, like in a game of chess, while in the olden days capital
was laid up by building a factory.[46] Lotteries and money games make
ordinary people rich as if by magic. From being a predictable amount
connected with work and production, money increasingly belongs in
inscrutable realms and takes unexpected courses. In many cases luck,
more than work, seems to be the appropriate explanation of someone's prosperity, thus undermining the hard work ethics typical of
Protestant societies. Payment cards and credit cards represent a new
abstraction of economy. Amounts of money circulate between
people and institutions without anyone ever holding a bank note in
their hands. Money is a sign on a transcript, not a treasure to be
touched.

Thus money is increasingly becoming an invisible stream of
energy in the world, corresponding more and more to the New Age
energy concept, and thus perhaps indirectly supporting a New Age
vision of the universe. Money, in its unpredictable, fluent, global and
abstract shape may be a more potent, religious symbol for our global
world of multiple systems than God the Father in his stationary, pre-
modern heaven. At the same time, the connection established
between money and human consciousness also makes it a personal
symbol. Thus New Age holism takes on a monetary dimension.
Wilde is expressing a vision of such monetary holism in the following passage:

46. Compare the following information from *Alternatives Economiques*: In
    1998 the average volume of daily transactions on the international ex-
    change markets amounted to 2000 billions of dollars, about 100 times
    more than the amount connected with trade in commodities and services.
    The equivalent amount in the 1970s was somewhere between 10 and 20
    billions. Cf. Chavagneux 1998, 31.

As I've said elsewhere in my writings, there are trillions of dollars zipping about electronically on any given day. Those electronic signals are literally passing through your body right now, as are all the TV and radio signals that are in your local area. If you stop and think about the millions flowing through your hands at the moment, imagine making a slight flick of the wrist in order to halt some of that loot in transit, so it sticks in the palm of your hand. A flick of the mind is faster than a flick of the wrist.[47]

The authors' discourse ignores how social class or economic structures in society may affect the possibilities of the individual. Poverty is seen as a condition created by humans relating to cosmic energies, and poverty is more or less unnecessary according to this way of thinking. You may create your own environment of abundance no matter what the economy around you is doing, Roman and Packer proclaim.[48] The combination of a cosmological and individualistic perspective prevents economic difference in society to be raised as a moral problem. Since abundance is inexhaustible and part of the energy flows of the universe, one does not take anything from others, or make them poor, by becoming rich. The idea is that prosperity is no limited cake to be shared; prosperity is an expanding process. Socialist solidarity is a non-topic; the basic orientation is individualistic and liberal. Old time Christian values like renunciation, poverty and sacrifice are out of the question along with discourse of sin and guilt. However, love, compassion and generosity are stressed, but most of all because it is good for oneself. The popular maxim that nothing enters a closed hand is fitting for this kind of ethic.

One could perhaps have expected that the cosmological vision would entail an ecological spirit, but the ecological dimension connected with economic growth and a rich life style is also ignored in this literature. The conception of the world in energy terms emphasizes its infinitude and immense power, while overlooking the vulnerability and limits of the eco system, replacing Gaia the vulnerable by a cosmic cornucopia. These social and ecological gaps in the dis-

47. 1998, 4.
48. 1988, xxviii.

course correspond with another significant gap, i.e. that desire is not always a positive human force.

Summary

Many factors in our time make economy mysterious and impenetrable, which, at least partly, can explain why cosmos speculations, magic, and spiritual self-development are gaining ground as economic wisdom and religious quest.

Globalization is involved in a range of issues in this account: the international diffusion of New Age literature and the corresponding impact of literary prophets as well as local reactions to books and ideas — in this case some Norwegian responses. Viewing globalization as a process involving meaning production, I have particularly focused on the construction of a cosmic-personal symbol system which transforms money into a spiritual symbol, consumers into enlightened beings, and see the world as their global horn of plenty. The spiritualization of prosperity reflects the values and discourse of a capitalist consumerism, which is becoming global in scope.

Bibliography

Beaudrillard, Jean 1999. 'Consumer Society'. In: Lawrence B. Glickman (ed.), *Consumer Society in American History*. Ithaca and London: Cornell University Press, 33-56.

Beck, Ulrich 2000. *What Is Globalization?* Cambridge: Polity Press.

Belsky, Gary and Thomas Gilovich 1999. *Why Smart People Make Big Money Mistakes — and How to Correct Them*. New York: Simon & Schuster.

Chavagneux, Christian 1998. 'Comment la finance est devenue incontrôlable'. *Alternatives Economiques*, 163, 28-31.

Chopra, Deepak 1993. *Creating Affluence. Wealth Consciousness in the Field of All Possibilities*. San Rafael: New World Library.

Chopra, Deepak 1996. *Suksessens sju åndslover*. Oslo: Hilt & Hansteen.

Dyer, Wayne W. 1996. *Ditt magiske liv. Frigjør dine iboende evner til å skape mirakler i livet ditt*. Oslo: Hilt & Hansteen.

Gillies, Jerry 1993: *Pengeglede. Tenk rikt! Bli rik!* Oslo: Hilt & Hansteen.

Glickman, Lawrence B. (ed.) 1999. *Consumer Society in American History: A Reader*. Ithaca and London: Cornell University Press.

Haaland, Hermund 1998. 'Han kalles "Dr. Increase": Motiverer til suksess'. *Dagen*, June 2.

Hanegraaff, Wouter J. 1996. 'New Age Religion and Western Culture'. In: *Esotericism in the Mirror of Secular Thought*. Leiden, New York, Köln: E. J. Brill.

Heelas, Paul 1992. 'The Sacralization of the Self and New Age Capitalism'. In: Nicholas Abercrombie and Alan Warde (eds.), *Social Change in Contemporary Britain*. Cambridge: Polity Press, 139-66.

Heelas, Paul 1993. 'The New Age in Cultural Context: the Premodern, the Modern and the Postmodern'. *Religion* 23, 103-16.

Heelas, Paul 1996. *The New Age Movement*. Oxford: Blackwell.

Hill, Napoleon 1998. *Tænk Dig Rig!* Søborg: Sphinx Forlag.

Holiman, James W. 1987. *Formelen til suksess*. Haugesund: Gemini.

Leland, John and Carla Power 1997. 'Deepak's Instant Karma'. *Newsweek*, October 20, 44-48.

Miles, Steven 1998. *Consumerism. As a Way of Life*. London: Sage.

Orman, Suzie 1997. *The 9 Steps to Financial Freedom*. New York: Crown.

Ponder, Catherine 1997. *The Dynamic Laws of Prosperity*. Marina del Rey, Calif.: DeVorss.

Power, Carla 1997. 'Chopra goes global'. *Newsweek*, October 20, 51.

Reibstein, Larry and Theodore Gideonse 1997. 'Don't Mess With Deepak'. *Newsweek*, October 20, 48-50.

Reigstad, Anne 1995. 'Gjeldfri med bibelsk hjelp'. *Bergens Tidende*, November 17.

Richardson, James (ed.) 1988. *Money and Power in New Religions*. Campeter: Edwin Mellem Press.

Roberts, Richard H. 1995. 'Power and Empowerment. New Age Managers and the Dialectics of Modernity/Post-modernity'. In: Richard H. Roberts (ed.), *Religion and the Transformations of Capitalism. Comparative Approaches*. London and New York: Routledge, 180-98.

Robertson, Roland 1995. 'Glocalization: Time-Space and Homogeneity-Heterogeneity'. In: Mike Featherstone, Scott Lash and Roland Robertson (eds.), *Global Modernities*. London: Sage. 25-44.

Roman, Sanaya and Duance Packer 1988: *Creating Money. Keys to Abundance*. Tiburon, Calif.: H.J. Kramer.

Shefrin, Hersh 2000. *Beyond Greed and Fear. Understanding Behavioral Finance and the Psychology of Investing*. Boston, Mass.: Harvard Business School.

Smart, Ninian 1996. *Dimensions of the Sacred. An Anatomy of the World's Beliefs*. London: Harper Collins.

Solum, Øyvind 1999. 'Deepak Chopra — guruen for bevissthet, helse og amerikanske rikfolk?' *Nettverk-Nytt*, 1, 77-78.

Tomlinson, John 1999. *Globalization and Culture*. Cambridge: Polity Press.

Wilde, Stuart 1998. *The Money Bible. Including The Ten Laws of Abundance*. London: Rider.

Waage, Peter Norman and Cato Schiøtz (eds.) 2000. *Fascinasjon og forargelse. Steiner og antroposofien sett utenfra*. Oslo: Pax Forlag.

CHAPTER 7

The Gnostic Myth and the Goddess Myth: Two Contemporary Responses to Questions about Human Identity

Ingvild Sælid Gilhus

Introduction

Generally, global systems challenge cultural and personal identities with the result that new identities are created, sometimes as revitalization of old ones. According to Peter Beyer, religious communication under modern and globalizing conditions 'addresses the problems that the dominant systems either leave out or create without solving'.[1] Questions about human identity pertain to problems which are of general cultural concern, but which the dominant systems do not solve. One of the places where questions about self and identity are discussed is in New Age texts and related literature.

The theme of this article is two contemporary religious myths about human identity, here labelled 'the Gnostic myth' and 'the goddess myth'. Both myths are preoccupied with creating meaningful identities, and both set voice to contemporary existential experiences concerning the human self. These myths focus on *eternal* aspects of human identity, but they are at the same time open for personal choice and inventiveness, and they use core symbols that are simultaneously universal and flexible. Thus they combine a cosmic dimension with a local and personal anchorage, a combination that is seen as both typical and necessary in a global religious situation.

---

1. Beyer 1997, 104.

The key examples of the myths in question are found in books written by American authors in the 90s. The books are *Crossing to Avalon* by the psychiatrist Jean Shinoda Bolen (1994) and *Omens of Millennium* (1996) by the literary critic Harold Bloom. Bolen's book combines general New Age ideas, goddess-religion and Christianity, while spiritualization and Gnosticism characterize Bloom's book. Like many similar books sold on the New Age market, *Omens of Millennium* and *Crossing to Avalon* are American, and like many of them, they are influenced by European religious ideas and have had a great European reception. A significant part of the European experience with new religions is the consummation of American New Age books, which are either translated into the national language or sold in their American version. There is, in other words, a transatlantic flight of religious ideas and a common literary circuit. In this flight, cosmic myths as the goddess myth and the Gnostic myth are localized and transformed to personal myths.

Globalization

In the case of the Gnostic myth and the goddess myth, we have a synthesis of European and American ideas. Bloom, for instance, is deeply indebted to the philosopher Hans Jonas who brought the existentialistic dimension of Gnosticism to the foreground. Bolen is dependent on the psychiatrist Carl Gustav Jung. Bloom combines Jonas with the American transcendentalist Ralph Waldo Emerson, while Bolen reinterprets Jung according to American feminism and goddess-consciousness. Globalization is about how the world has shrunk, potentially at least, to one social system, and into one global room where things and thoughts are flowing. But ideas, identities, and things have always been sent across countries and continents. Globalization as such describes continual historical processes of integration.[2] What is new today though, is the technological impetus and speed in which changes occur. Global flow may trigger a search for fixed orientation points.[3] The Gnostic myth and the myth of the goddess are examples of attempts to establish such points. In the new

2. Cf. Robertson 1998, 183; Warburg 1999, 40f.
3. Meyer and Geschiere 1999, 2.

transatlantic globalization, the divine is drawn *into* man, as part of human identity, and the religious universe tends to develop within the sphere of human consciousness. In a way, this development can be seen as a democratization of religion and the end-product of religious processes which were initiated in antiquity when the human being became a preferred vehicle of the sacred, a development which culminated in antiquity with the birth of Christianity.[4]

Both Bolen and Bloom are using Christian myths in their religious projects. Both authors connect wisdom and spirituality to the symbolic power of the past in ways that make the past enchant the present.[5] The construction of an ideal past interpreted as a spiritualization and a synopsis of a variety of ancient religious myths is dependent on a crystallization of the category of religion.[6] It is also dependent on the use of that type of religious material which was originally adapted and edited by the history of religions and made accessible to a wider audience. Both the goddess myth and the Gnostic myth exploit and abundantly use religious material which has been adapted by the history of religions.

Omens of Millennium

In *Omens of Millennium: The Gnosis of Angels, Dreams, and Resurrection*, Harold Bloom, professor of literature at Yale, has written a witty and polemical book where he presents his religious convictions as a sort of gnosis. Bloom describes gnosis as a spirituality, which is directed towards the innermost core of the soul, a core that is part of the fallen Godhead. One of his points is that Americans have in the last two centuries sought God within themselves, rather than the God of European Christianity. As stated in an earlier book, *The American Religion: The Emergence of the Post-Christian Nation*, Bloom views America as fundamentally Gnostic, and the Church of Jesus Christ of Latter-Day Saints as its most characteristic religious project.

---

4. Gilhus 1999.
5. According to Roland Robertson, 'we are currently in a new phase of accelerated, nostalgia-producing globalization' (Robertson 1998, 158).
6. Beyer 1998.

In *Omens of Millennium*, both the good God, who is estranged and exiled, and a fallen God appear. But they are pale figures that do not inspire much, neither do they fascinate nor frighten. For Bloom's text is not primarily about God, it is about the human self. Man is shut off from God and deeply polarized. Three parts make up his being: The innermost part which corresponds to the highest God; the *psyche* or soul which corresponds to the intermediary realm of images; and the body through which man is tied to the material world.

The inner self is eternal, not created, and cannot die. This deep self is connected with a feeling of transcendence, a transcendence that for Bloom was opened up by reading. The act of salvation is to distinguish the psyche or soul from the deep self, a realization which implies that the deep self is identical with God. This realization of identity between God and self is an act of gnosis, simultaneously to know God and being known by God:

Gnosis depends upon distinguishing the psyche, or soul, from the deep self, which pragmatically, means that any strengthening of the psyche depends upon acquaintance with the original self, already with God (Bloom 1996, 22-23).

The deepest self is no part of nature, or of history; it has no matter or energy. Consequently, it does not act. This self can only be acted upon and reached through the *psyche*, which is the most intriguing part of Bloom's concept of man. This concept is enriched by means of myths and images from the different traditions that Bloom has brought together, such as Zoroastrianism, Gnosticism, hermetism, kabbalah, and Sufism. The mythological brew makes the category symbolically rich, but also ambiguous. Through ancient religious texts and modern imaginative literature, human beings may encounter the inner self and reach out towards God: 'Knowing myself, knowing Shakespeare, and knowing God are three separate but closely related quests'.[7]

Bloom's focus on the spiritual dimension of human beings, excludes discussion of bodily and gendered aspects of human life and also of how human beings are connected to the world at large. It re-

7. Bloom 1996, 14.

sults in a rather one-sided anthropological construction where the processional, ritual and ethical aspects of men and women's existence in the world are little developed. Institutional and social religious life seems to play a small part. The stress is on the eternal characteristics of man, independent of cultural and historical circumstances. *Omens of Millennium* is not the testimony of a mystic. Bloom is more of an esoteric adept: The wordless union between God and self gets less praise than creative fantasy and images of the soul.

The Past and its Possibilities

As mentioned, Bloom ties his Gnostic quest firmly to the past, represented by hermetism, Christian Gnosticism, Shiitic Sufism and Jewish kabbalah. These movements are not easily accessible and their texts are difficult. Bloom leans on authorized translations and indisputable expertise — Garth Fowden on the Hermetic corpus, Hans Jonas and Bentley Layton on Gnosticism, Henry Corbin on Sufism and Gerschom Scholem on kabbalah. Frequently, the texts Bloom has chosen lack their original institutional and social contexts, and their origin and mutual connections, if there are any, remain largely unknown. For example, we do not know the origins of Christian Gnosticism, and little about who the Gnostics were and how they worshipped. The Hermetic texts lack their original context and audience. A connection between the ancient Gnostics and the medieval Cathars is at best a possibility. Precisely in this lack of historical knowledge, openings and empty spaces appear that give ample possibilities for creating new relationships and significant spiritual connections.

When Bloom associates himself with the Gnostic traditions within certain world religions, he momentarily obtains into the bargain the richness of three western world religions. In a way we can say that he both 'has his cake and eats it too'. He partakes in the traditions of the world religions, at the same time as he chooses what is often seen as their esoteric and so-called heretical parts and thus disassociates himself from the mainstream variants of these religions, but which, of course, have been absolutely necessary for these traditions to have existed at all. He then proclaims the esoteric parts to be the most original and genuine. Bloom's strategy on this point is very similar to what other actors on the new religious scene do.

In doing this, Bloom seems to overlook how religions consist of immensely rich webs of traditions and thus are more like tapestries than balls of string. During time they are woven again and again, new threads are put in, old ones are unravelled, and some older threads are hidden by the new. Therefore, usually it is neither possible to find any beginning, which is *the* beginning, nor an original motif, which is more basic than other motifs.

In *Omens of Millennium*, the origin of Gnosticism is found in Judaism, as well as in apocalypticism and shamanism. With an ancient origin goes a venerable past, which implies authenticity and depth. For that reason, almost everyone who acts in the world of religions wants an ancient past. In Bloom's view, the past is also qualitatively better than the present. The ancient texts have given him a profound religious inspiration, and he wants to establish a spiritual standard. In his own words: 'Without a context that can serve as a spiritual standard of measurement, we will drown in New Age enthusiasm and wish fulfilments'.[8] Bloom measures current religious phenomena against the best that was written about them in the past, and finds the ancient texts to be of infinitely higher quality than the new ones. The Gnosticism of the past, being more spiritual, was purer than that of the present. As well as an ancient past, a spiritual self in man has also automatically guaranteed depth. It suggests wisdom and a rich inner life — mystics and adepts in esoteric traditions have often had high status.

Even if Bloom is scornful of New Age, his credo reflects religious tendencies which are similar to those we find in New Age: to focus on self, to see the human being as spiritual, and to interpret the processional and material side of the human condition more like an outer covering or a shell, not to be mistaken for the real person. Also in legitimating his view by references to the past, Bloom resembles New Age authors. Furthermore, a parallel between Bloom's religious universe and that of New Age is the accentuation of fantasy and imagination as legitimate approaches to religion. However, this is partly in contrast to the ancient Gnostics, many of whom saw the fallen creation as an expression of divine fantasies and images run wild. We recall the Valentinian Gospel of Truth and how Error (*plane*) made

8.   Bloom 1996, 74.

images and substitutes for the truth and thus became the source of the material world. So, when Bloom went out to detect the inner self in man and was fascinated by its fantasizing alter ego, the soul, his project is not so much in consonance with ancient Gnosticism as it is with the modern religious scenario where fiction and novels are royal roads into the very heart of religion.

The most original part of the Gnostic inventiveness was perhaps the concept of original man identified with god, the ultimate apotheosis of man made according to the divine image. This image seems also to have been that which has especially fascinated Bloom in Gnosticism. It represents a profound wish that the centre shall hold even if the periphery is disintegrating. This identification between the inner core in man and the divine is an answer to the search for one solid point that makes human existence meaningful. In this point one image, one self and one truth meet. Meaning is monistic, but it is given only by draining the experience of being-in-the-world of ultimate significance.

Bloom's Gnostic myth with its stress on spirituality and transcendence is one answer to the question of man's identity. It can be compared with another contemporary anthropological construction, which is also set in a universal and cosmic context, namely the goddess.

Crossing to Avalon

The goddess is one of the most original contemporary religious developments. In the vicinity of the goddess, spirituality is embodied and the female body made sacred. She is a flexible symbol found in traditional- as well as in new religions, in organized- as well as in diffused religion, in theology ('thealogy') as well as in psychology and art. One of her abodes is the contemporary novel.

Jean Shinoda Bolen, a Jungian analyst and clinical professor of psychiatry at the University of California, is a spokeswoman for the goddess. Bolen has written several books, best known is probably *Goddesses in Everywoman* (1984), a bestseller, which has had its ideas reproduced in women's magazines around the world. Her recent book, *Crossing to Avalon: A Woman's Midlife Pilgrimage*, reflects a spiritual quest in the form of a travel to sacred sites, the chief of them being Glastonbury in England. Stories from modern fantasy literature and mythological literature of different ages are interwoven with the thrill of sacred places, personal religious experiences, and dreams. As we have seen in the case of Harold Bloom, creative imagination where literature and religion meet and fuse is one significant aspect of contemporary religiosity. And even if the design of Bolen's tapestry is personal, the patterns she uses are not. The main themes are typical for our time and age: focus on self and self-development, how to tackle personal crisis, the status of the body, a religiosity that is gendered.

Bolen's pilgrimage is characterized by individual choice and inventiveness. Many sacred places are visited, many spiritual persons met. Christian pilgrim sites as the Cathedral of Chartres, are combined with New Age sites. Dalai Lama appears in the text as well as the present Archbishop of Canterbury and a Hindu religious leader. A mythological past is evoked; and one of the chapters is, with allusion to Chaucer, called 'Glastonbury Tales'. In *Crossing to Avalon*, the *sacred* works through the earth, wells, stones, churches — and, not least, through the female body. Not only do selected bodies partake in the *sacred*, but also all female bodies.

The Sacralization of the Female Body

When matter and the female body are sacralized, holiness is bestowed on something that is changeable and perishable. In the cult of saints in the Middle Ages, their dead bones and other relics were preferred vehicles for the sacred. These relics were unchangeable, a witness to an ideal of bodies made static. The physical resurrection of the body was a basic assumption of medieval religious thought, continuity of the body a precondition for the continuity of the self. In our culture, the unchangeability of the body is not connected to an immortality gained through death — the expectation of new life beyond the grave is diminished or nil. The ideal of an unchangeable body is connected to this life and eternal youth. Slimming, gym and advertising bear witness to this ideal, and a body that is forever young and beautiful is its primary icon. The cultural fixation on the female body is something mainstream culture and goddess spirituality has in common, but their direction of focus is opposite. Goddess spirituality focuses on the processional body, while mainstream culture's idealization of woman focuses on unchangeability.

The unchangeable body of the young female is ideal and unattainable, a product of media transmission. It is body made into an object, a body that is on display and transmitting a message, which is identical with its surface. In opposition to this dominant image of the female body in mainstream culture, in Goddess spirituality, the body has become a subject. It is *me* and *mine*. It is processional, and its three phases as maiden, mother and crone are sacralized. The female body is described by Bolen as overflowing, generating, babies, milk and blood — a horn of plenty for such stuff as life is made of, which implies that the body's inherent capacity to bear and nurture is focused upon. Its sacredness is connected to every woman, and thus sacredness has become a subjective category as well as a female quality.

In Bolen's Goddess spirituality, the centre of the female body is not its head and cerebral part, but the chest, which virtually is the body's middle point. Women sense in their bodies, and bodies are organs of memory. This corresponds to how the Goddess' symbolic organ is the womb and knowledge is connected to her heart, which is a physical expression of how stress is laid on the body's life-giving, caring and nurturing functions. Accordingly, the female body becomes the primary foundation of knowledge.

When women and female bodies are brought into the centre of religious attention, the opposition between change and duration is also an issue. The laws of change rule bodies, and these laws are made into a main religious dynamic. An important prefix in Bolen's text is *re-*: the goddess re-emerges, the holy Grail re-turns, the ancient rituals are re-membered, goddess religiosity is re-discovered, the past is re-gained, the planet is re-sacralized, women are re-minded of their past by re-telling Arthurian legends, love between two women is a re-union. This use of the prefix *re-* implies a return to a past that was better and more authentic, and this return heralds at the same time a renewal. By going back, the present is made fresh and full of new life. Repetition gives eternity to that which changes. Goddess spirituality is not concentrated on that which is unique and has happened only once, as the birth, death and resurrection of Jesus. Instead it is concentrated on that which alters but always is the same. Processional female bodies become durable points in reality because they participate in an eternal return. While change in the form of ageing is a main problem in Bloom's book, change in *Crossing to Avalon* is connected to female biological processes more than to the process of ageing.

The Sacralization of Gender

It is a clear tendency in *Crossing to Avalon* to make the mind/body problem an aspect of gender. This has, of course, been a tendency in Christian history through the centuries. But gender is not only connected to the polarity of mind/body. Other polarities are also drawn into the context of gender, and Goddess spirituality is on several points an inversion of Christian values as they have usually been practiced by the organizational mainstream, for instance when it comes to the polarity between subject/object, soul/body, male/female, authority/individuality, death/birth.

A gender polarity is a way to give energy to culture. This could partly explain why simultaneously as it has been a strong drive in Western culture for more than a century to make men and women equal, counter processes will also appear that accentuate gender differences. Because sex divisions are more blurred today than they were in earlier times, attempts to make new demarcations appear. Goddess spirituality is one way to emphasize a new gender polarity and to make the female into its most sacred part. Everyday experiences and biological processes generate a sacredness that seeps virtually into every pore of the female body. Behind the goddess and the spiritualization of gender lies a Jungian psychology that gives spiritual, psychological and biological legitimacy to the ruling social relationships between the sexes, but which in this case tries to turn them into a source of female power. When the female gender is made into a spiritual depth dimension, a new gender hierarchy is created.

Paradoxically, parallel with the female biological sphere being sacralized in goddess religion, this sphere is invaded by technology and opened up for choice in mainstream culture. Family planning, new techniques of contraception, abortion, postponing of menopause, artificial insemination, post-menopausal women giving birth, breast surgery etc. This technical and medical revolution does not seem yet to be a main concern of the Goddess, at least not in *Crossing to Avalon*. Though, it could be said that this is what the Goddess implicitly opposes. The sacredness of the female body is an innate quality. It is not due to those technical and medical regulations that contribute so intensely to construct contemporary female bodies. It is not the body produced by surgery and artificial hormons that is made sacred, it is body as an eternal creation of nature, mediated through the consciousness of the Goddess.

In Bolen's text the narrative moves between belief and fiction, the eternal and the changeable, the archetypical and the personal, myth and history. This sort of locomotion is rather typical in contemporary new religions. The past evoked by Bolen is an imagined past, played with and situated within the psyche as well as encountered in stones and buildings. The past is in the present, and the symbolic power of ancient traditions and classical myths are used to enchant women's experiences today. The global situation, where the world is one place, is extended to include the past, which in this way becomes one dimension of globalization. In this weaving together of past and present, the personal stories and the universal story confirm each other, and individual experiences are made sacred.

Both in Christianity and in Goddess spirituality, religious meaning is intimately intertwined with the human body. But in contrast to Christianity, where texts get their meanings from the dead and risen body of Christ, we have seen that in Goddess spirituality, the female body and its gender related processes are the anchorage for symbols, myths and experiences. Meaning is not restricted to a unique body, a master body, as it is in Christianity, but to all female bodies.

Localization

The Gnostic myth of the exiled spirit and the goddess myth, are flexible myths, both when it comes to a capacity to include a variety of mythical material and to their ability to be applied by individuals in their lives. These myths are met on three levels — cosmic, local and personal. With an expression borrowed from the historian of religions Irving Hexham and the anthropologist Karla Poewe, I will describe such myths as box-myths. According to Hexham and Poewe, box-myths are 'myths within myths that enable people to place them-selves within a cosmic framework'.[9] These authors say that the 'par-ticular box-myth making that attracts contemporary new religionists is that of creating a personal myth within a cosmic myth'.[10] Individ-ual mythmakers universalize particular experiences by linking them to existing myths, or to fragments of myths, that are universal. They also 'particularize universal myth fragments by living them out as their own experience'.[11] This model of myths, conceived of as boxes, can be applied to the Gnostic myth and the goddess myth.

These myths are cosmic in the way that they relate humans to the grand scheme of things, to the exiled god or to the universal goddess, respectively. Cosmic myths can be localized as well as being person-alized. The Gnostic myth has, for instance, got a local formulation when American religiosity is described as Gnostic, as Bloom does. The cosmic Gnostic myth can also give rise to personal and individ-ual myths. In the Gnostic case, it includes a specific Bloomian narra-tive as a personalized Gnostic myth.[12]

As for localization of the goddess myth, in Bolen's book, there is a significant box stuffed with Arthurian mythology, written from a feministic perspective, and placed in Glastonbury in England. The book itself, *Crossing to Avalon*, can be described as Bolen's personal goddess myth.

It seems also to be a characteristic of the modern mythological box-systems, not only that they have boxes within boxes, but also that the boxes are easily transferred from one system to another. A box can, for instance, be taken from the system of Gnostic myths, and transferred to the box system of goddess myths. When Bolen, refers to the Gnostic Sophia, a Gnostic box is put into the goddess system.

How are the Gnostic myth and the goddess myth received in Europe, in this case in Norway? Do they inspire local myths? Are they turned into personal myths? *Yes*, but at the present time they are used only to a lesser degree as the basis for organizations. Their modi vivendi are as personal myths.

9. Hexham and Poewe 1997, 167.
10. Ibid. 69.
11. Ibid. 74.
12. Mikaelsson 1999.

The Gnostic myth is, for instance, found as a personal link to the world of literature and art. One of the leading Norwegian dramatists, Jon Fosse, has recently written a book with the title, *Gnostiske Essay* (Gnostic Essays). Fosse's understanding of Gnosticism, inspired by Bloom, is that literature can be a source of Gnostic truth and an individual knowledge of God. This implies that the best literature reflects a looking for the lost God. Language has a religious dimension; it separates human beings from God, as well as making a connection between them and Him. In Fosse, the link between religious and literary transcendence is made, and a nihilistic outlook, seen in his earliest texts, has gradually been changed for a new actualization of the divine.[13] Fosse is influenced by literary theory, as found in Walter Benjamin and Derrida, with their anchorage in Jewish mysticism and kabbalah, but in Fosse, secularized literary theory has now been resacralized.[14] In the words of Fosse, 'And for me the novel is, to say it stubbornly, constantly on the track of the lost God' ('Og for meg er romanen, for å seie det påståeleg, stadig på sporet av den tapte Gud.').[15] It is not so peculiar, that Bloom's ideas about Gnosticism, for instance 'that literary works can communicate transcendence',[16] has found a response in Fosse.

Jon Fosse is not the only Norwegian artist who has been inspired by Gnosticism. Another example is the professor in figurative painting at the Norwegian Academy of Art in Oslo, Jan Valentin Sæther. He is also a priest, ordained in Los Angeles, in *the Ecclesia Gnostica* (which has only a handful of members in Norway). Sæter was recently interviewed in a journal called *Alternativt Nettverk* (Alternative Network). This journal is about what moves, (and wants to move) on the contemporary new religious scene in Norway. It is published every other month. In this interview, Valentin Sæther tries to profile Christian Gnosticism in relation to Christianity of the Church. One of

13. Hverven 1999.
14. Hagerup 1997.
15. Fosse 1999, 46.
16. Bloom 1996, 20.

his points, is that the Church through history has tried to control art and the human imagination. Sæther says that Gnosticism to a higher degree than the church has managed to take care of creativity and to preserve a spiritual tradition.[17]

In addition to these intellectual receptions, Gnosticism in Norway also appears as part of goddess religion with basis either in neo-paganism or in Christian female spirituality. These forms of Gnosticism, like Jon Fosse's and Jan Valentin Sæther's, seem in their Norwegian context also to have got a direct and contemporary inspiration from America.

As for goddess religion in Norway more generally, it mainly takes the direction of a Christian mysticism on the fringes of the Church inspired by the models of the two Marys (the mother of Jesus and Mary Magdalene). But there are also examples of a goddess spirituality more in the direction of Paganism, which tries to include old Norse goddesses such as Idun, Freya and Hel. In addition, there are types of Scandinavian shamanism which draw inspiration from the old Norse goddesses, and where the Sami shaman, the *noaide*, may be seen as fulfilling the same functions as the old Norse seer, the Völve.[18] In Norway, myths about Norse goddesses are used as links between individuals and the cosmic myth of the goddess. To my knowledge, it is primarily ad hoc groups that exist at present rather than stable organizations.

The Gnostic Myth and the Goddess Myth — A Comparison

In the Gnostic myth and the goddess myth, we meet the idea of a universal human identity, which transcends everyday experience. We also meet the need to create new differences as part of that universal identity. I think both myths pose gendered questions. Bolen's underlying question is the meaning of being a woman, presupposing that to be a woman has cosmic significance. Bloom's question is more like: What is the ultimate purpose of man's life? (presupposing that there is a ultimate purpose). In this question, man is apparently a non-gen-

17. Solum 1998, 80.
18. Høst 1994.

dered category, but seems all the same to require a certain male identity. Bloom's remarks about New Age — which is 'a panoply wide
enough to embrace Shirley MacLaine and Mrs. Arianna Huffington, in
which Ms. MacLaine worships Ms. MacLaine (with some justification)
and Mrs. Huffington reveres Mrs. Huffington (with perhaps less)'[19] —
suggests, among other things, an unmistakable male bias.

Bolen's use of the female body reflects a dominant tendency in
goddess spirituality, namely to criticise and turn away from what has
been labelled a Platonic quest for disembodied forms. Thus we see an
initial difference between Bloom's and Bolen's religious projects.

Feminist historians and philosophers characterize the symbolic
underrating of motherhood as an important key to patriarchal power.
Emphasis is laid on how all people are born of women: '*Woman* is the
stuff out of which all people are made', says the historian of religions
Naomi Goldenberg.[20] This is also Bolen's point. Curiously, the stress
on the material aspect of birth partly echoes Aristotle who emphasized how the male contributed form to the foetus while the female
contributed matter. In Aristotle's view this division between the sexes meant a devaluation of the female. In goddess spirituality, the sacralization of woman and matter is an inversion of Aristotelic values.

Bloom's Gnostic myth has something directly to say to the study
of literature and to creative work, which we also saw in the case of
Jon Fosse and Jan Valentin Sæther. Bloom's bid on power is to the
power of an intellectual elite. Bloom's myth is further about the
United States as the heir of ancient Gnosticism: 'Authentic spirituality in the United States, for nearly two centuries now, is essentially
Gnostic'.[21] In Bloom's hunting after an authentic self, meaning is
found out of this world, everything is in a fallen state and almost
nothing lives up to expectations. Bloom laments what has been, and
his Gnostic myth is tragic. In comparison, Bolen's myth is optimistic.
One reason for this could be that the goddess myth is more processional than Bloom's myth.

19. Bloom 1996, 17.
20. Goldenberg 1995, 154.
21. Bloom 1996, 229.

Bloom's and Bolen's books are written for a broad audience, in accordance with how one general tendency in New Age is to democratize the sacred and make it accessible for everybody. At the same time, their religious projects have elitist aspects, which I also see as typical for the contemporary scene. Bloom and Bolen invite their readers to choose an identity according to taste and need. Generally, a spiritual interpretation of religious myths and texts makes them, on the one hand, universally valid and therefore suited to a global religious market. On the other hand, a spiritual interpretation tends to establish religious elites and support elitist thinking. Bloom connects religious traditions which have in common the fact that they are difficult to interpret. He sees them as belonging to ancient religious elites and as catering for the eternal spiritual aspect of human beings. His enthusiasm for ancient Gnosticism is accompanied by an attack on popular religious ideas as the belief in personal angels and near-death-experiences. Perennial philosophy is thus held up against contemporary religious commercialism. True Gnosticism is, in Bloom's thinking, a literary religion, a religion of an elite.[22]

But in spite of Bloom's message being intended for an elite, paradoxically, the structure of his argumentation is rather vulgar. Like much religious prose with a wish to convert, Bloom's text is permeated by polarities: The past contra the present; institutional, historical and dogmatic oriented religion contra a religion ruled by imagination and creativity; American contra European Christianity; believers in the God of Holocaust contra Gnostics at heart; Bloom's spirituality contra New Age. These polarities reflect Bloom's wish to convert his audience, his style is that of a preacher: The final chapter of *Omens of Millennium* is called 'A Gnostic Sermon'.

We find a similar ambiguity in Bolen as in Bloom whether the message is for the chosen few or for everybody. Apparently Bolen is more of a religious democrat than Bloom. But only *apparently*. The highlights of her pilgrim tour, not least her meetings with the Dalai Lama and the Archbishop of Canterbury, most definitely make her religious quest a first class journey; a de luxe pilgrimage. Bolen's pilgrimage and ideas of the goddess probably speak directly to a sector

22. Ibid., 33; 182-83.

of contemporary upper middle-class feminism. Bolen implies an identity acquired through travels, courses and books. This is an identity that usually costs money, and thus requires purchasing power.

The goddess myth presupposes woman consciousness of a type that could conveniently be called cosmic feminism. *Crossing to Avalon* fits into a broader field of novels and magazines that transmit cosmic feminism as a wider cultural reservoir, operating independently of institutionalization. Whether this cosmic feminism is a sidetrack when it comes to women's real competition for power and influence is another matter. In Norway, for instance, there is a certain interest in books about cosmic feminism. Books like Bolen's clearly have an audience. These books are noncommittal and are part of a non-organized religiosity where religion is entertaining. That there seems to be less interest in organized goddess groups in Norway can be due to the fact that feminism in the Scandinavian countries has been part of the political agenda for years. It could be questioned if the influence of political feminism in Scandinavia makes cosmic feminism less attractive and less necessary as the ideological foundation of organized groups.

A Global Self

Underlying both the Gnostic myth and the goddess myth are questions about human identity. One of the features of postmodernism and the global context, is a decentring of the subject.[23] Contemporary men and women live with the 'identity problem' unsolved.[24] And even if it were a strongly felt need to attain an identity for oneself, to have a fixed identity for life would be a handicap.[25] If it is true that the late modern self appears more like a process than a state, and that this process has a certain open-ended character with no fixed goal, personal creativity and dynamism would be necessary and sought after qualities. The late-modern self is constructed in a world where people, technology, money and information are continually in flux, and to be successful, the self must also develop this quality.

23. Featherstone 1995, 44.
24. Bauman 1997, 26.
25. Ibid., 24-26.

The question of the self is closely related to the question of the status of the body. The relationship between soul and body reveals a tension between a wish for holism on the one hand, and rootedness in dualistic thinking on the other. This tension is nourished by an opposition between New Age, which as secularized religion is aiming at immanence, and New Age dependency on traditional Western religions, which are aiming at transcendence. This opposition leads to conflicts, compromises and unresolved problems. Holistic thinking is strong in relation to new concepts of the body and the earth. Dualistic thinking is expressed when the spirit within is given absolute value. Bolen chooses the first option, Bloom the second.

The goddess myth and the Gnostic myth open up doors to the global religious market where religions and traditions exist with infinite possibilities for input to the process of creating a self. When people are invited to relate creatively and dynamically to various religious traditions and mythologies, the symbol of the goddess or the symbol of the exiled soul/exiled God are structuring these traditions and mythologies in a meaningful direction, giving them a focus.

These myths represent countermoves against routinization and bureaucratisation, which reduce human beings to numbers in statistics and to anonymity. As countermoves, they offer strategies for making the self whole, potent and free — on a spiritual level. In these myths, imaginative spaces are created, confined spheres, within which human beings are set free from the control of society, but this human liberation happens mainly in the realm of images and phantasy.

Two different types of self are implied in these myths. One is a self in flow, a changeable self that is never fixed, fitting the changing identities and roles of the late modern person. At the same time the shimmering surface of a world in flux could imply lack of depth. There is a longing for a permanent point, for that which will never melt into the air, for a centre. Such longing is, as we have already seen, reflected prominently in Bloom's Gnostic myth. To construct a permanent self may be a strategy for imagining depth. Perhaps this sort of self or identity can only exist as a transcendental possibility? Consequently, a self is flow and a monistic self are two types of constructions to be discerned in the symbols, images and myths of late modern religiosity. How they are combined differ. While Bloom is more interested in an eternal deep self and to distinguish the self from the psyche, which is flexible, Bolen finds permanence and a sort of eternal return in the cycles of the processional female body. Thus the goddess myth and the Gnostic myth reflect different versions of cosmic nostalgia and offer two different answers to the question of human identity both as a global and as a personal phenomenon.

Bibliography

Bauman, Zygmunt 1997. *Postmodernity and its Discontents.* Oxford: Polity Press.

Beyer, Peter 1998. 'The Religious System of Global Society: A Sociological Look at Contemporary Religion and Religions'. *Numen*, 45, 1-29.

Beyer, Peter 1997. *Religion and Globalization.* London: Sage.

Bloom, Harold 1993. *The American Religion: The Emergence of the Post-Christian Nation.* New York: Simon & Schuster.

Bloom, Harold 1996. *Omens of Millennium: The Gnosis of Angels, Dreams and Resurrection.* London: Fourth Estate.

Bolen, Jean Shinoda 1984. *Goddesses in Every Woman. A New Psychology of Women.* New York: Harper & Row.

Bolen, Jean Shinoda 1995. *Crossing to Avalon: A Woman's Midlife Pilgrimage.* New York: Harper.

Featherstone, Mike 1995. *Undoing Culture. Globalization, Postmodernism and Identity.* London: Sage.

Fosse, Jon 1999. *Gnostiske Essay.* Oslo: Samlaget.

Gilhus, Ingvild Sælid 1999. 'Nye religioner i hellenistisk-romersk tid og idag. Kritiske spørsmål til komparasjonens mulighet'. In: P. Bilde and M. Rothstein (eds.), *Nye religioner i hellenistisk-romersk tid og i dag.* Aarhus: Aarhus University Press, 24-38.

Goldenberg, Naomi 1995. 'The Return of the Goddess: Psychoanalytic Reflections on the Shift from Theology to Thealogy'. In: U. King (ed.), *Religion & Gender.* Oxford: Blackwell, 145-63.

Hagerup, Henning 1997. 'Harold Bloom og Gnostisismen'. *Samtiden*, 2/3, 41-43.

Hexham, Irving and Karla Poewe 1997. *New Religions as Global Cultures: Making the Human Sacred.* Boulder, Colo.: Westview Press.

Hverven, Tom Egil 1999 'Ikkje tilstrekkeleg vekt til liv'. *Syn og Segn*, 1, 58-71.

Høst, Annette 1994. 'Om kvinnekraft, kretsløp og spirituelt arbeid'. *Alternativt nettverk*, 5, 16-18.

Meyer, Birgit and Peter Geschiere (eds.) 1999. *Globalization and Identity: Dialectics of Flow and Closure*. Oxford: Blackwell.

Mikaelsson, Lisbeth 1999. 'Selvbiografien som personlig myte'. In: B.G. Alver, I.S. Gilhus, L. Mikaelsson and T. Selberg (eds.), *Myte, Magi og Mirakel i Møte med det Moderne*. Oslo: Pax, 75-96.

Robertson, Roland 1998. *Globalization: Social Theory and Global Culture*. London: Sage.

Solum, Øyvind 1998. 'Gnostisisme, kristen mystikk og erfaringen av det hellige'. *Alternativt nettverk*, 1, 4-7; 76-80.

Warburg, Margit 1999. 'New Age og gamle dage. Religion og globalisering i dag og i hellenistisk-romersk tid'. In: P. Bilde and M. Rothstein (eds.), *Nye religioner i hellenistisk-romersk tid og idag*. Aarhus: Aarhus University Press.

CHAPTER 8

The Myth of the UFO in Global Perspective: A Cognitive Approach

Mikael Rothstein

Introduction

The myth of the 'flying saucer' and the subsequent narrative of the so-called Unidentified Flying Objects (UFOs) came into being in the aftermath of World War II and thus in a period of time when modernization was well underway. According to many recent studies, modernity is understood to be a transnational social process and therefore it is of no surprise that religious or semi-religious ideas typical to this period — such as the UFO myth — tend to spread into many different areas of the world. The globalization thesis, on the other hand, is primarily concerned with the emergence and development of new sociological patterns rather than distribution of ideas: According to sociologist Peter Beyer, the phenomenon of globalization refers to a situation where 'people, cultures, societies, and civilizations previously more or less isolated from one another are now in regular and almost unavoidable contact' (Beyer 1994, 2). The 'unavoidable contact', whether political, economic or cultural, seems to be at the heart of the globalization phenomenon. In this paper, however, my focus shall be on the communication of religious or semi-religious ideas rather than cultural 'contact' in more general terms. I shall also restrict my analysis to one single theme as it has appeared during a relatively short period of time, although globalization as such is often perceived as a long-term historically rooted process 'that helps to form new patterns of global interaction, new global institutions, and new ways of thinking about the world as such' (Lechner 1998, 209).

What I am about to discuss is the international spread of the UFO myth; its origins and some of the premises that allowed it to grow, differentiate, and become one of the modern world's most powerful religious or semi-religious narratives. In doing so I shall apply theories of communication derived from cognitive science, especially the work of American anthropologist Dan Sperber. How this relates to the study of New Age religion will be discussed in the following.

Religious Groups — Religious Ideas

Religious movements, whether heavily institutionalized or just emerging, will often display strategies of world dominion and thus ambitions of global presence. While such ambitions in themselves are no direct sign of globalization, the fate of the missionaries' work will be determined by the prevailing socio-cultural conditions. In a situation where globalization, as characterized above, is a reality, the spread of single religious movements (whether modern or ancient, see Warburg 1999) is a more probable phenomenon compared to a situation where the general socio-cultural exchange is much weaker. The relatively modest success of such groups, however, shows that a globalizing socio-cultural environment in itself does not do the trick. A group may be present in many countries and cultures at the same time, but presence is not necessarily the same as influence or real success (Rothstein 1996).

Things may be very different regarding the distribution of religious ideas (rather than organizations). Ideas travel faster and more easily than organizations, and the uncontrolled flow of ideas is not bound by the same kinds of social structures as those administered by this or that religious group. New Age cosmology, in the broadest sense of the word, can in many ways be seen as part of such a flow. It is correct, of course, that New Age concepts very often are intimately linked with organizations or may be attributed to specific individuals, but New Age ideas are usually distributed outside the direct control of particular organizations or influential individuals. People take part in an informal network, either by engaging themselves directly in New Age activities or simply by orienting towards New Age perspectives — consciously or not. This lack of institutionalization probably explains why New Age thinking has gained such a relatively high momentum. The boundaries are loose and the possibilities countless.

Notions of UFOs and what grows out of this image are an increasingly popular element in many people's tentatively composed New Age cosmologies. The notion of the UFO, though, originated outside the realm of New Age thinking and in order to understand its way around most of the world and into a more or less globalized New Age philosophy, we shall have to start somewhere else.[1] In essence the idea of the UFO has split into several different traditions, and the New Age related understanding is one of them. Starting with the Theosophically inspired 'contactees' of the 1950's, who claimed to have direct contact with superhuman, benevolent extraterrestrials resembling the Mahatmas or Adepts of classical Theosophy, New Age concepts on the subject have developed in many different ways. Sometimes New Age notions on alien visitation or interplanetary travel are rooted in older traditions (Emanuel Swedenborg is important in this connection), but the main impulse to contemporary New Age ideas on UFOs are the evolutionary pattern of Theosophy as advanced by the contactees. Today, however, the 'nuts and bolts' understanding of the UFOs of the 1950's is declining, and a more versatile way of interpreting the alleged phenomenon has come up; the UFOs are still around in New Age theologies, but they rarely land as they used to, and people rarely meet face to face with the occupants. Rather, channelling and astral body travel have become commonplace as a means for communicating with the superhuman beings. The image of the UFO has become part and parcel of an overall New Age cosmology based on ideas of evolution, and the long term fate, as well as the imminent future of Mankind, has been linked with beings from other planets. The very idea of the UFOs has become far more important than sightings, landing marks, photographs or other sources that would allegedly document the actual existence of the objects people claim to have seen. In New Age terms the UFO has become a spiritual category, a dogma that needs no proof. In fact many people use

1. A much more detailed discussion on this subject is found in Rothstein 1999 and 2000.

the idea of extraterrestrial contact, one way or another, as their point of spiritual departure, as one of the basic assumptions in their religious demarcations.[2]

In sociological terms the kind of informal religious networking that constitutes the New Age movement has been labelled an 'audience cult' by sociologists of religion Rodney Stark and William Simms Bainbridge who states that 'cult audiences' rarely meet physically, and that partaking in cult related activities almost remains a consumer activity. People are, so to say, imbibing cult doctrines almost entirely through impersonal communication (Stark and Bainbridge 1985). The common interest in UFOs, whether rooted in secular ufology or New Age metaphysics, similarly could be seen as some type of audience cult. In choosing such a perspective, the different kinds of believers in UFOs are lumped together with only one common reference: They all believe in the existence and occasional presence of extraterrestrial intelligent life forms. Talking of globalization and UFO mythology it is this extremely variegated audience cult that comes into focus.

The emphasis in the following, however, will be on the historical and social developments that lead to the introduction and distribution of the UFO as a cultural representation — the developments that went ahead of the subsequent New Age oriented interpretation and use of the UFO image. In terms of globalization it is important to observe that the very notion of the UFOs was globalized before the current popularity of New Age religion, and that the spread of New Age concepts in this respect therefore must be understood as a second phase in the globalization history of the UFO image.

2. It is worth noting that the number of reported sightings has been steadily decreasing for quite a number of years — even if beliefs in UFOs is as high as ever. Prior to 1977, for instance, the British UFO Research Association (BUFORA) recorded about 300 sightings a year. In 1985 the number was 20 (Randles 1993, 87). Increasing sophistication of witnesses and investigators may account for the drop, but it is also possible that the notion of UFO has become routinized to such a degree that sightings are no longer necessary to uphold the UFOs as public representations.

The Origin of UFO Mythology

The notion of UFOs has changed considerably since the concept of 'flying saucers' was coined in American news media in the summer of 1947. It all started when people learned of a strange incident involving private pilot Kenneth Arnold (d. 1984). After a flight on June 24, 1947 over the Cascade Mountains in the State of Washington, Arnold reported that he had encountered nine strange, flying objects. Talking to a local newspaper reporter about his experience, he explained that the objects held a tremendous speed and that they moved 'like a saucer would if you skipped it across water'.[3] Arnold was referring to the movements of the objects but a headline editor had it (deliberately or not) wrong, and the notion of 'flying saucers' was subsequently presented to the public.[4] Kenneth Arnold's description of the objects, though, was in fact quite unlike 'saucers': He described them as 'crescent shaped', a fact rarely mentioned in popular UFO literature.

In the wake of the local media coverage during the days following Arnold's sighting, other newspapers, covering a much wider geographical range, carried the story, and a growing number of witnesses came forward with new reports: Apparently 'flying saucers' had been spotted in many different places — but curiously enough mostly in the areas where Arnold's story had been mentioned in the newspapers. Some witnesses even claimed to have seen the strange aerial objects several days or weeks prior to Arnold's experience. Nobody but Arnold, though, implied that they had seen crescent shaped objects manoeuvring in the skies. On the contrary, what people claimed to have seen, were saucer shaped objects. The public obviously responded according to the image conjured up in the media coverage which repeatedly referred to 'flying saucers'. The image of the 'flying saucer' had in a matter of days or weeks become a cognitive model for how subsequent sightings (whether grounded in some kind of

3. John Spencer, 1991, 31.
4. According to British ufologist John Spencer, the very term 'flying saucer' is only known to have been used once prior to 1947, when a Texas farmer, in those words, described an object allegedly seen over his farm in 1878 (ibid. 147-48).

real experiences or deliberate fantasy) should be interpreted and reported. During the following months the story spread, and within a short time it could be identified virtually everywhere in the United States and in many parts of Europe, including the Soviet Union. In the years to come the stories of the 'flying saucers' would develop, and, as far as New Age religion is concerned, merge with a whole range of mythical, metaphysical and religious traditions to which the concept originally did not belong.

From the very beginning the concept of 'flying saucers' grew out of a highly fascinating tale brought to the public's attention through different media reports. In people's reading about the strange objects, the 'flying saucers', whatever they actually were, became *social* facts. Those inclined to respond to the media coverage very often adopted the stories as true, but nobody was able to ascertain the actual nature of the alleged phenomenon. As a matter of fact the understanding that the 'flying saucers' were alien space ships did not surface in the public until almost three years after Arnold's sighting.[5] In other words: at the outset of the modern flying saucer myth, we find a specific narrative — and not much more than that. What was to become an international mental epidemic started as a local media event, and what happened during the weeks following Arnold's sighting was a forerunner to developments on an almost global scale. According to a Gallup Poll from 1987, 88% of the American population had some awareness of UFOs, and 9% claimed that they themselves had seen something strange in the skies. About 50% of the sample asked believed UFOs to be 'real objects' rather than constructs of human imagination. These figures were quite similar to what investigators found to be the case ten years earlier, and the figures are almost the same today.[6] A recent Swedish survey by sociologist of religion Ulf Sjödin revealed that more than 25% of the adult population have a firm belief in, or at least positive attitude to, the existence of UFOs and extraterrestrial visitations to Earth, and figures from other Scan-

---

5. For further details see Rothstein 1999, where I have tried to explain some of the reasons why the unidentified flying objects were soon to be interpreted as spacecrafts from other worlds.
6. John A. Saliba 1995, 15.

dinavian countries show the same pattern.[7] Statistics are harder to obtain from other countries in the world, but many things point to a similar status in Russia and other former Soviet republics. UFOs are reported from all over the world — currently with as many stories from Japan, France and South Africa — although the stronghold of popular UFO stories remains the United States. At any rate, the UFO myth has become an international narrative with an impact upon the lives and thoughts of thousands and thousands of people. But why and how? Presumably a religious idea needs to have some kind of global appeal in order to spread into many different countries. What then could cause a global attraction in the late 1940's and early 1950's when the UFO myth came into being?

Cold War Fears and the Globalization of the UFO Myth

According to folklorist Robert Pearson Flaherty the original 'flying saucer' rumours and later developments cannot be understood apart from the overall political and cultural conditions of those days — the Cold War. As the conflict between East and West was building up, people realized that their lives and the very existence of Mankind, was under permanent threat, and the psycho-social climate became more and more difficult. In every thought and every action ordinary people had to take into consideration that a devastating atomic war could break out. In the light of the unwillingness or inability of the political authorities to curtail the proliferation of nuclear weapons, says Flaherty, 'there arose a myth of extraterrestrials prepared to either prevent nuclear destruction, or assist a surviving remnant' (Flaherty 1990, vi). The flying saucer, according to this theory, serves as a symbolic mediator between the two oppositional powers, but also as a mediator between the individual and the complex society of which he or she is a tiny part. Flaherty shows convincingly how the flying saucer myth in principle holds the very same features that are known from the traditional myths of Christianity; a descending sa-

---

7. Ulf Sjödin 1998, 51-74. There may be no connection, but it is curious to note that the number of people in many European countries who believe in reincarnation is of the same magnitude.

viour who puts an end to suffering and conflict, provided people are willing to follow him. The central observation, however, is that the notion of the 'flying saucer' is a collective representation of widely shared concerns in popular culture. 'Widely', in this connection, soon came to mean international and even global. From the earliest phases in the history of the UFO myth the idea spread to the Soviet Union where the myth apparently was at work as early as 1949. Indeed one of the earliest UFO writers, retired Marine Corps major Donald Keyhoe, in his book from 1950 *Flying Saucers are Real*, notes that the strange crafts are also seen in the Soviet Union (Keyhoe 1950, 131). The phenomenon was apparently a matter for the two superpowers that were more involved in the Cold War than any other nations. The perspective appeared over and over again in popular culture. In Robert Wise's widely circulated film *The Day the Earth Stood Still* from 1952, for instance, this concern of Americans as well as Russians was a central theme: In this film a visiting alien in a space ship advocated the abolition of nuclear weapons on Earth, a suggestion he was prepared to enforce: Either we on Earth live in harmony, or we would be destroyed (Flaherty 1990, 243). In the following years UFOs were reported from all over the world: In Australia and New Zealand public knowledge of the phenomenon only got underway in the middle of 1950, South Africa followed immediately after, South American countries joined in the early 1950's, and then Europe and subsequently Japan. In Muslim countries, however, the reports were extremely few — and they still are today. Put very briefly, UFOs seem to be spotted primarily in countries or lands where American culture is influential one way or another.

A Cognitive Approach

Why 'flying saucers'? What properties are contained in this specific image that may explain why it was widely accepted as a potent symbol during troubled times, and why does it still work? Obviously there cannot be one single answer, but some of the principles behind the image and its global popularity may be uncovered by means of cognitive science.

According to anthropologist Pascal Boyer, who approaches the religious creativity of humans from the field of cognitive science, a prime characteristic of religious ideas and experiences is that they entertain 'counter-intuitive' elements. These elements transcend universally acknowledged ideas of the world and the categories that structure it — the ordinary intuitive ontologies — which, says Boyer, makes them excellent tools for thought and reasoning. Because such ideas are 'attention demanding' people are able to remember a myth or another type of sacred (i.e. counter-intuitive) narrative better than mundane descriptions of 'ordinary things'. On the other hand, no religious system is entirely composed of counter-intuitive elements. On the contrary. According to Boyer, most religious systems will primarily rest upon an intuitive ontology of the world and the counter-intuitive or 'supernatural' dimensions will in fact be few. Some kind of ontological balance is needed, and too strong emphasis on counter-intuitive representations may prove fatal for a religious discourse. The cognitive categories that structure the ideas of the world, whether shared collectively or upheld by an individual, cannot be too attention demanding. Nonetheless, it is precisely the attention demanding, counter-intuitive elements that make extra potent meaning in specific situations possible: The Christian narrative of how Jesus was convicted and crucified, for instance, displays no counter-intuitive elements, but decisive counter-intuitive dimensions are added in the subsequent myth of the resurrection (Boyer 1994, 1994a).[8] The UFO myth, then, may be seen as yet a balanced story of counter-intuitive events or phenomena: The notion that UFOs come from another world may not in itself be a counter-intuitive idea, but the fact that they transcend normal categories such as time and space takes them into the realm of counter-intuitive elements. UFOs move in absurd or impossible ways, they fluctuate between different dimensions, they emit light rays that stop in mid air, they often appear in elusive dreams or cognitive twilight zones etc. etc. In this sense it is perfectly possible to see UFOs as religious images. What we need to discover is what kind of 'thought and reasoning' they provide, what kind of 'memories' they carry and maintain. Considering the fact that the 'flying saucers' entered the arena during the early years of the

8. The section (on intuitive and counter-intuitive beliefs) is taken from Rothstein 1999.

Cold War there is no reason why the cognitive approach should not support the thesis presented by Robert Pearson Flaherty; that the UFOs originally were born as a response to Cold War fears, and that the symbol subsequently, in the diverse New Age context, has taken on a line of different epistemological and soteriological implications. In the Cold War scenario the UFOs appear as mediators, as agents for non-human intervention during a situation where an atomic holocaust was a real threat. In the later New Age context the UFOs are signs of super-human, divine presence, and thus symbols of higher levels on the evolutionary ladder that form the core dimension in most New Age thinking.

In terms of globalization, the interesting point is that the cognitive approach may explain why people in many different parts of the world have responded in very similar ways to the same narrative. The answer is in fact simple: According to cognitive theories, humans respond in very much the same way to basic cognitive impulses. Transcending intuitive ontology, therefore, means more or less the same everywhere. Accordingly, narratives of strange crafts that perform impossible things in the air are by their nature accessible for further interpretation. The 'flying saucers' were subjected to all sorts of interpretations, but the basics of the narrative were the same in every understanding — the kind of counter-intuitiveness involved did not change: Kenneth Arnold himself, for one, was inclined to believe that the strange objects he saw in the sky were unknown animals living at high altitudes, but as his story was communicated it took on many different attitudes. In the years following the first flying saucer reports there was no consensus regarding the nature of the phenomnon. On the contrary, the years following 1947 were characterized by great confusion and lively discussions. People hypothesized that Soviet agents were infiltrating the United States by means of flying saucers, others believed secret government agencies to be responsible or that surviving Nazi groups hiding under the ice cap of Antarctica were preparing an assault on the United States. Another theory was that of visitors from inside the Earth, but most people simply did not know what to believe (Clarke and Roberts 1990, 19-25). The notion that 'flying saucers' were the vehicles of visiting aliens from other worlds was not present from the beginning. Indeed the terms 'flying saucer', 'flying disc' and 'UFO', which eventually came to mean 'extraterrestrial spacecraft', have changed in meaning over the years. Anthropologists Benson Saler and Arthur Ziegler say: 'In 1947 few people linked these terms to extraterrestrial visitations, whereas by 1992 a majority of Americans considered the terms to be synonymous for "alien spaceship"'. They also point to the fact that the gradual change in the meaning' of these terms was paralleled by the creation and growth of a UFO community, i.e. 'individuals linked by a common espousal of the extraterrestrial hypothesis as an explanation for some of the thousands of UFO sightings reported over the years' (Saler et al 1997, 13). As it appears, the public idea of the UFOs grasped by the audience cult of Stark and Bainbridge, was nourished by the thoughts and ideas of a far smaller group of UFO enthusiasts that had come together to solve the enigmas of the alleged phenomenon.[9]

Wherever the myth has gone, it has been interpreted according to local conditions. The reports from India are remarkable examples that often will link UFO observations to traditional Hindu myths of the vehicles of the gods, the *vimanas* (Thompson 1993), some American Hopi Indians have linked UFOs to their traditional religion (Geertz 1992, 287) and several Christians groups have taken the UFOs to be angelic beings, demons from hell or a means for transporting the dead to Heaven (Rothstein 1997). At other times people have taken the UFOs and their occupants to be the same phenomena and creatures that we are told about in pre-industrial European folklore. In every case it is clear that the interpretation is linked to local traditions, either geographically or ideologically. It is a fact, for instance, that UFO occupants all over the world are described in very different terms, but that each description relates directly to local traditions, ethnical boundaries, local presumptions etc. (Skjelborg 1979). In short it seems as if the image of the counter-intuitive UFO and what follows has struck a cord with a general, i.e. global, cognitive appeal, and with good possibilities for various kinds of local interpretations.

But in what ways, more precisely, are religious ideas transmitted. What are the actual mechanisms at work during a distribution such as the one previously described? Other aspects of cognitive science offer a suggestion.

9. For further discussions, see Rothstein 1999.

'The Epidemiology of Belief'

Aiming at a more precise way of discussing matters of belief and re-ligious imagery, cognitive scientists will usually label specific reli-gious beliefs as different kinds of 'cultural representations'. One such cultural representation may be belief in witches, another belief in one god or many gods or indeed in the existence of 'flying saucers'. Such representations — in order to be 'cultural' — are widely shared in a human group. According to anthropologist Dan Sperber, this means that explaining cultural representations is to explain why some rep-resentations are widely shared (Sperber 1997, 82). If the representa-tion 'UFO' could be explained we should, following Sperber, also be able to understand its global distribution.

Sperber distinguishes between two kinds of representations that, when coordinated in specific ways, form the collectively shared cul-tural representations of a given group. One category is what he terms 'internal' or 'mental' representations; 'for example, memories, which are patterns in the brain and which represent something for the owner of that brain'. The other category is the 'external' or 'public' representations; 'for example, utterances, which are material phe-nomena in the environment of people and which represent some-thing for people who perceive and interpret them' (Sperber 1997, 78). Sperber holds that public representations are more basic than mental ones because 'meaning — the regular relationship between that which represents and that which is being represented — is social be-fore being individually grasped' (Sperber 1997, 79). The young child does not discover the world unaided, and then make public or pri-vate representations of it, he says. On the contrary most representa-tions of the world — and what is contained herein — 'are acquired vi-cariously, not through experience, but through communication or through a combination of experience and communication' (Sperber 1997, 78-79). One important thing about public representations (such as the concept of UFOs) is that they gain all their meaning from either their producers or users. Public representations have no semantic properties of their own. When the public representations concern ob-jects that only exist as concepts in the minds of people, this fact is even more obvious. UFOs, as ideas rather than physical facts, for instance, can only have the meaning attributed to them by the producers or users of the concept (Sperber 1997, 81).

It goes without saying that any distribution of ideas requires communication, which means that distribution or globalization is in itself a process of communication of public representations. It is commonly acknowledged, says Sperber in this connection, that communication is a kind of 'coding process' followed by 'a symmetrical decoding', and it is assumed that 'replication of the communicator's thoughts in the minds of the audience is the normal outcome of communication' (Sperber 1997, 83). This, however, is not the case according to Sperber and Deirdre Wilson. Together they have argued that a process of communication is basically one of transformation (Sperber & Wilson 1998): 'the degree of transformation may vary between two extremes: duplication and total loss of information', says Sperber, and emphasizes that 'only those representations which are repeatedly communicated and minimally transformed in the process will end up belonging to the culture' (Sperber 1997, 83).

The case of the UFO is an example of such a representation. Since 1947 stories of UFOs have been told and retold, and although many changes have taken place during its move into every corner of the world, the basic components of the narrative are present in virtually every local variety of the myth. During the same period of time the level of cultural communication has increased tremendously. We have seen how the 'flying saucers' were born as a narrative in the news media, and since then the numbers of books, films, journals, pictures, broadcasts, and most recently — but highly significant — Internet pages on the subject have been growing and growing, thereby increasing the availability of what Sperber calls 'external memory stores', which, so to say, serve as keepers of a given public representation.

This supports and stimulates the existence of the myth. The fact that no UFO has been put on display means that people, when addressing the issue of UFOs, never perceive the object they themselves believe to talk about. The actual existence of the UFOs is in people's communication about them, in their publicly shared representations of their own representations, so to say. The more external memory stores available, the more this kind of communication will be possible. The globalization of mass media therefore provides very good opportunities for a continuous global consolidation and ramification of the UFO narrative. The fact that the majority of the populations in most Muslim countries remain outside the immediate reach of Western mass media, may thus explain the absence of UFOs in local narratives and the fact that stories of UFOs by and large remain a feature of Western culture.

In ways similar to Boyer, Sperber further distinguishes between 'intuitive beliefs' and 'reflective beliefs'. The idea that 'God is everywhere', for instance, is a reflective belief which according to Sperber, like most religious beliefs, 'does not lend itself to a final, clear interpretation, and which therefore will never become an intuitive belief' (Sperber 1997, 90). The fact that people may accept such a reflective statement as true (that this particular god exists and that it is everywhere), is due to specific structures of authority and power. There is no way of testing the statement, but it can be believed because it is communicated by a certain source of authority. Stories of UFOs are transmitted globally by different kinds of sources, each with its own kind of authority; individual witnesses, media reports, organizations, authors, military agents etc. The phenomenon allegedly observed and communicated, will usually only be half-understood and therefore open to reinterpretation. In other words: the idea of UFOs is communicated with authority, but it is those receiving the communication that have the final power of attributing the kind of meaning to it they prefer. The UFOs' consistency or inconsistency with other beliefs, intuitive or reflective, is never self-evident, and does not provide a robust criterion for acceptance or rejection (Sperber 1997, 91).[10]

In order for a narrative such as the UFO myth to serve as a dynamic cultural mechanism, a relatively large proportion of a population needs to know it, and two conditions must, according to Sperber, be met: 'First, the story must be easily enough and accurately enough remembered on the basis of oral [or written] input alone [...]. Second, there must be enough incentives to actually recall and tell the story on enough occasions to cause it to be transmitted' (Sperber 1997, 95). As we have seen this is indeed the case with the UFO narrative. The

10. This is quite similar to what Boyer calls 'undertermination'.

fact that the content of the myth has drifted over time only means that it has maintained maximal memorability. Psychological conditions of memorability and attractiveness are met, and the story has become well distributed. However, many people who know the basic elements of the UFO myth do not believe in it; they see it as a tale. According to Sperber this is due to the fact that the authority structure is more fragile than the transmission structure (Sperber 1997, 96). The story is told and remembered, but not necessarily believed.

In this sense stories of UFOs come in two distinctively different types; as a myth which is believed, and as a tale which is not. Considering the UFO myth as a believed story, i.e. as a religious narrative, New Age cosmologies have nourished it for the past decades and taken it into new realms. I would thus hypothesize that the further global distribution of the myth has much to do with the overall syncretistic nature of New Age beliefs and the ability of New Age religion to engage positively with many, many different religious systems around the world. Indeed this is supported by Sperber and others when they state that in order to become a success a religious representation has to be open to interpretation, it has to be flexible. The less specific it is, the better the possibilities for survival and development. The image of the UFO is just that: elusive, flexible and versatile and therefore an obvious candidate to become a global cultural representation distributed along the ever-expanding means for easy international communication.

Bibliography

Beyer, Peter 1994. *Religion and Globalization*. London: Sage.

Boyer, Pascal 1994. 'Cognitive Constraints on Cultural Representations: Natural Ontology and Religious Ideas'. In: Lawrence A. Hirschfeld and Susan A. Gelman (eds.), *Mapping the Mind. Domain, Specificity and Culture*. Cambridge: Cambridge University Press, 391-411.

Boyer, Pascal 1994a. *The Naturalness of Religious Ideas*, Cambridge: Cambridge University Press.

Clark, Jerome 1992. 'The Emergence of a Phenomenon: UFOs from the Beginning through 1959'. *The UFO Encyclopedia*, Vol. 2. Detroit: Omnigraphics.

Clarke, David and Andy Roberts 1990. *Phantoms of the Sky. UFOs —
A Modern Myth*, London: Robert Hale.

Geertz, Armin W. 1992. *The Invention of Prophecy. Continuity and Meaning in Hopi Indian Religion.* Knebel: Brunebakke Publications.
(Special Danish Edition by agreement with The University of California Press).

Keyhoe, Donald 1950. *Flying Saucers are Real.* New York: Fawcett
Books.

Lechner, Frank J. 1998. 'Globalization'. In: William H. Swatos (ed.),
Encyclopedia of Religion and Society, London: Altamira Press, 208-9.

Randles, Jenny 1993 (1987) *The UFO Conspiracy.* New York: Barnes &
Noble.

Rothstein, Mikael 1996. 'Patterns of Diffusion and Religious Globalization. An Empirical Survey of New Religious Movements'.
TEMENOS, Vol. 32, 195-220.

Rothstein, Mikael 1997. 'The Family, UFOs and God. A Modern Extension of Christian Mythology', *Journal of Contemporary Religion*,
Vol. 12(3), 353-62.

Rothstein, Mikael 1999. 'The Rise and Decline of the First Generation
UFO Contactees. A Cognitive Approach'. *TEMENOS*, Vol. 35, 2000.

Rothstein, Mikael 2000. *UFOer og rumvsener. Myten om de flyvende tal-
lerkener.* Copenhagen: Gyldendal.

Saler, Benson, Charles A. Ziegler & Charles B. Moore 1997. *UFO Crash
at Roswell. The Genesis of A Modern Myth.* Washington: Smithsonian
Institution Press.

Saliba, John A. 1995. 'Religious Dimensions of UFO Phenomena'. In:
James R. Lewis (ed.), *The Gods Have Landed.* Albany: State University of New York Press.

Sjödin, Ulf 1998. 'Tror vi på det dolda?'. In: Owe Wikström (ed.), *Att
se det dolda.* Borås: Natur och Kultur.

Skjelborg, Åge 1979. *På sporet af ufonauten*, Copenhagen: Berlingske
forlag.

Spencer, John 1991. *The UFO Encyclopedia.* London: Headline Books.

Sperber, Dan 1996. *Explaining Culture. A Naturalistic Approach.* Oxford: Blackwell.

Sperber, Dan & Deirdre Wilson 1998. *Relevance: Communication and
Cognition*, (second edition). Oxford: Blackwell.

Stark, Rodney and William Simms Bainbridge 1985. *The Future of Religion: Secularization, Revival and Cult Formation*. Los Angeles: University of California Press.
Thompson, Richard L. 1993. *Alien Identities. Ancient Insights into a Modern UFO Phenomenon*. San Diego: Govardhan Hill Publications.
Warburg, Margit 1999.'New Age og gamle dage. Religion og globalisering i dag og i hellenistisk-romersk tid'. In: Per Bilde and Mikael Rothstein (eds.), *Nye religioner i hellenistisk-romersk tid og i dag*. Aarhus: Aarhus University Press, 39-52.

CHAPTER 9

'Going Global from the Inside Out':
Spiritual Globalism in the Workplace

Karen Lisa Goldschmidt Salamon

Most of the Earth's population is touched by a trend of modernist homogenization in terms of identity quests, industrial consumerism and commercialization. Ethnic and cultural fragmentation has not prevented the systematic spread and homogenization of capitalism across borders and continents.[1] Threats of nuclear warfare and environmental destruction affect humans on a global scale, and no one can entirely 'opt out' of the transformations brought about by modernity.[2] A complex system of integrated world trade and communication has been in existence for more than a century. An open, international economy involving significant transnational investments of capital and massive exchange of goods across continents is thus not a recent phenomenon. The globalization of the economy has risen in total figures, as the total *amount* of transnational trade has grown (and fluctuated) massively during the past hundred years. In relative terms, however, economic globalization was as significant prior to the First World War. The economies today do not seem to export or import significantly more — proportionally to their GNPs — than they did a hundred years ago.[3] Since even further back in time colonialism and imperialism have interconnected 'human aggregates' across the Globe.[4] The assumption that globalization is a recent phe-

1. Friedman 1990.
2. Giddens 1991, 22.
3. Hirst 1997, 14ff.
4. Wolf 1982.

nomenon thus appears to be wrong in systemic, economic terms. However, influential techniques of everyday functionality have spread across most continents since the end of the Second World War and the introduction of the *pax Americana*. Technical standards and academic research methods are transnationally regulated and converged, and the formats of mass media, popular musical trends and communication systems are homogenized. However, this process does not necessarily imply a globalization of social structures, cultural (p)references and icons of meaning. Even though finance is global, most people of the Globe have no access to any sort of investments. And where armed conflicts draw their technological resources from global arms markets, most of the killings remain local issues involving very limited transnational concern or intervention. With certain reservations as to the novelty and social diffusion (to the less privileged) of globalization, it is thus possible to argue that we today are facing a single 'global system' in terms of a 'world society [that] has reached a higher level of complexity with higher structural contingencies, more unexpected and unpredictable changes [...] and, above all, more interlinked dependencies and interdependencies'.[5]

Observed from a constructed extra-planetary perspective, such as that of the observing sociologist quoted here above or from the 'astronaut's angle of vision', or from that of the 'prophet',[6] the transregional interactions might add up to a whole global system, in which all parts are mutually dependent. However, it is also possible to argue that this 'global system' is a theoretical and social construction and a matter of ideological references and cosmology. Both positions might be argued together, as they relate to different ontological levels.

Global-*ism*

We need to consider that most of the significance and novelty of globalization stems from its articulation as a central point of reference in national and corporate political strategies and cultural identifications of the 1980s and 1990s. My concern here is with a particular version

5. Luhmann 1997, 75.
6. Barnet and Cavanagh 1994, 420.

of this articulation. The transnational elites, and those hoping to become such, have turned into self-reflexive globalizers, identifying
themselves in terms of their belief in The Global. Globalization has
become a goal and cultural icon in itself, often detached from its functional and operational aspects. In this article I am concerned with a
particular variety of 'the world imagined as a globe'[7] — global-ness
and globalization — as ideological references and icons of belief. I
have chosen to discuss this Global-*ism* in terms of an ideological position. It articulates itself as a rather commonsensical cultural adaptation to indisputable facts of globalization. I want to question the ob-
viousness of this construction, and view it as a specific cultural phenomenon worthy of further study. I find it semantically paradoxical
that individual, earthly identity and happiness are articulated in
terms of a global consciousness and existence, when actual 'life is
lived at such close proximity to the earth's surface that a global perspective is unobtainable' (for anyone who happens not to be an astronaut).[8] I have chosen to discuss a particular version of this *Globalism*.
It is an ideological formation that intersects business strategies and
management ideology with new forms of spirituality and a strong
belief in a single global system and world-society. The formation is
produced by a number of business consultants, entrepreneurs, management academics and corporate managers in their writings, social
rituals and organizational strategies. I want to argue that these
people attempt a re-articulation of business to an individual spiritual
pursuit of global dimensions. This re-articulation takes place mainly
through a re-definition of the workplace in spiritual terms.

7. Ingold 1993, 31.
8. Ibid., f. Among other issues leading to the dominance of the global image,
    Ingold discusses modern visualism and detachment as scientific posi-
    tions privileging the external, global gaze over local life-knowledge and
    internal perspectives. 'The image of the world as a globe is, I contend, a
    colonial one. It presents us with the idea of a preformed surface *waiting to
    be occupied* [...]' (op.cit. 38). The image also evokes ideas of a world exter-
    nal and prior to all the life forms of Earth, whereas the Earth in fact con-
    sists of all that lives and grows here. Thus Western images of the globe
    have construed human society as external to the Earth and the 'physical
    world', thus making it possible for us to 'manage' and 'own' it. Non-
    western and pre-modern conceptions of the world place humankind *in-
    side* the world.

New Managerial Teachings for Ever More Competitive, Transnational Work Markets

The president of the management-consulting firm *Livelihood* of Santa Fe, New Mexico, Martin Rutte, writes:

The nature and meaning of work are undergoing a profound evolution. Two forces are helping to catalyze the momentum of this process — fear and the emergence of both a more personal and widespread spirituality. The fear is about losing our job and having to do more with less. And the emergence of spirituality in the workplace points to the desire that there be more to work than just survival. We yearn for work to be a place in which we both experience and express our deep soul and spirit.[9]

9. Rutte 1998.The definition of 'spiritual' in this and the other texts I study here remains rather open. Following ethnographic tradition, I let the informants and practitioners of the field define the central concept of their ideology, rather than trying to conclude on a single, synthetic meaning of the concept, as seen from the 'outside'. Definitions differ from convinced belief in 'common consciousness' and higher spiritual orders as inspirational sources to managers (cf. Salamon 2000a), to less metaphysical, more Human Potential inspired understandings. A representative of the latter is president of *Livelihood*, a management consulting firm in Santa Fe, New Mexico, Martin Rutte, who writes thus about spirituality in the workplace: 'The journey is *not* about spirituality as 'the answer', but about spirituality as 'the question'. A question allows you to look more deeply. It allows you to search for what's true for you, and in so doing, deepen your own experience. But ultimately, what moving from answer to question does is make it safe and permissible to explore this territory in a way that is useful. What is spirituality for you? Where is spirit or spirituality not showing up in your workplace? Where is it flourishing? Explore these kinds of questions, at work, for yourself, your relationships, your division and your company. And in this questioning, in this exploration, notice the deepening of your own experience of spirituality at work. [...] What would a more spiritual workplace mean for people? It would mean that work would move from merely being a place to get enough money to survive — from just earning our daily bread — to being a place of *livelihood*. By livelihood I mean a place where we both survive and are fully alive' (Rutte 1994).

Martin Rutte is one of a number of more or less influential business development consultants, who since the 1980s have shown growing concern for so-called *values based management*, in particular making workplaces and business-management wiser, more spiritual[10] and ethically principled. These consultants — and a number of business practitioners — have introduced concepts usually associated with religious traditions — such as *path, mission, vision, preacher* and *spiritual intuition*[11] — to the world of annual reports,[12] internal corporate training,[13] strategy and marketing.[14] *Values based management* speaks in

10. See e.g. http://www.spiritatwork.com/,"Helping to Envision and Create the Enlightened Workplace". And 'ReGenesis Associates, Organizational transformation through individual transformation', (http://www.spiritat work.com/regen/2000).

11. Jørgen Bonde Eriksen, director of the Intuitive Business Institute, Denmark, first introduced the concept Intuitive Leadership to me. The structured and formalized use of intuition in business management practice seems to have begun in the United States with inspiration from the Human Potential Movement, as have most of the spiritually inspired techniques in management discussed here. 'If people would use just 10% of their intuitive ability, we'd have better organizations and happier people. Intuition is really nothing more than using all aspects of your intelligence to run a business better. Although intuitive knowledge often seems to be hidden and obscure, once you learn how to tap into it and listen to its wisdom, innovative ideas will flow with a rush like the water over Niagara Falls', says Sandra Weintraub, President of Management Resources in Newton, MA, in an interview with Tom Brown (1999). She claims that companies such as Quaker Oats, Reebok, and American Greetings have made management decisions based on intuition.

12. E.g. the engineering consultancy Ramboell, Denmark that describes itself as a holistic enterprise (http://www.ramboll.dk/ramboll/pub/dk/htm/generelle/holistisk).

13. See e.g. Thrift 1997.

14. A conspicuous example of this is Danish advertising agent Jesper Kunde, who uses holistic and religious concepts for explicitly operational purposes. In his 1997 marketing manual *Corporate religion — the path to a strong business* he writes: 'The main goal of a Corporate Religion is to strengthen and regiment the efforts of the enterprise — no matter at which market it attempts to sell its brands. This makes a Corporate Religion into a holistic outlook — and an ideological outlook' (Kunde 1997, 13).

favour of creating a general, overall sense of purpose in organizations and having employees imbibe particular cultural values. Particular ideological guidelines diffused amongst employees are believed
to keep employees loyal and corporate identification strong.[15]

British business consultants *Richard Barrett & Associates LLC.*
write:

> In an age of increasing global competition, human creativity, personal pro-
> ductivity and social responsibility are becoming the new frontiers of compet-
> itive advantage. The ability of an organization to build a corporate culture
> that attracts and retains the best people, and supports employees in their per-
> sonal and professional development is rapidly emerging as the number one
> criteria for financial success.[16]

Thus, new managerial teachings and practices generally acknowldge
that the continued creation of economic value depends on their ability to create and organizationally maintain particular modes of symbolic production and cultural references. They accordingly focus on
methods for creating and maintaining a stable organizational identity
and solid loyalty from employees whilst keeping the workforce flexible and the organization-structures fluid in ever more competitive,
transnational markets.

Spiritual Values at Work

The growing concern for ethics, human rights and environmental issues amongst customers has furthermore provoked managerial concern with values, ideology and ethics as corporate guidelines. Issues
of *trust* — between customers and corporations as well as inside organizations — are addressed, and spiritual advisors and retreats for
managers are introduced. Management is prompted to make em-

---

15. 'In the 1980s, consultants told managers to base decisions on logic, data,
    and cold, hard facts. In the millennium-crazed 1990s, decision-making
    has gone decidedly New Age, with recent books by so-called "intuitive
    consultants" telling us to enrol in the Jedi Knight School of Management'
    (Dahle 1999).
16. *Richard Barrett & Associates LLC* 1998.

ployees actively seek spiritual self-development and self-knowledge.[17] This strand of *values* concerning management knowledge is
mainly produced in North America and Britain, but also in some of
the large, industrialized Latin American countries and continental
Europe. It appears to draw inspiration from Asian management theory such as Japanese production-systems, classic eastern religious
traditions[18] and from European romanticist ideals.[19] Furthermore
elements of American Puritan traditions, modern New Age spiritualism[20] and other contemporary syncretic movements plus Gestalt
psychology, Human Potential and similar holistic[21] approaches are

17. In this movement it is generally accepted that the inner development of
    individuals (self-development) must preclude communal and societal
    progression. Evolution happens 'from the inside out' (Salamon 2000a).
    See also p. 162 of this Chapter.
18. Several management writers today refer to Buddhism and other eastern
    traditions in their discussions of ideal leadership. The highly influential
    consultant and management academic, Peter M. Senge of Innovation As-
    sociates and Sloan School of Management, quotes Lao Tsu in a discussion
    of leadership skills and tools (Senge 1992, 93). There are several books —
    probably reaching a more limited audience — on Western adaptations of
    Eastern thought applied to management, such as *Zen and Creative Man-
    agement* (Low 1993) and *The I Ching of Management* (Sadler 1996).
    Amongst more 'mainstream' readerships, inspiration from Japanese
    management has been very widespread in the 1980s and 1990s. The very
    influential management consultant and academic Peter Drucker discuss-
    es Japanese decision-making as 'highly effective. It might, therefore, be
    fruitful to take a look at the Japanese way of decision-making [...]'
    (Drucker 1977, 374). Inspired by among others Sony co-founder Akito
    Morita and consultant Kenichi Ohmae, Japanese management concepts
    and production systems such as that of Toyota are by now broadly used
    in western management discourse. *Muda*, supposedly meaning 'waste',
    kaikaku, which is said to mean 'instant revolution' and *kaizen*, 'continuous
    improvement' are used in the original Japanese, untranslated form in the-
    ories on the creation of quality (Bicheno 2000).
19. In Salamon 2000a, I mention this in relation to figures of authenticity.
20. Cefkin 1998 mentions empowerment movements and New Age in rela-
    tion to 1990s corporate practices and visions. See also Salamon 2000b.
21. Harrington 1996 discusses the modern history of the holistic concept and
    ideologies linked to this.

recognisable to various extents. Besides drawing its inspirations globally and thematically addressing issues related to globalization, it also sells globally. Spiritually inspired approaches to work and business-management have been widely broadcast since the early 1980s, partly by the breakthrough of non-academic management-books. These paperback, 'airport bookstore' type books are published in tens- or hundreds- of thousands of copies in several languages, and distributed partly by the Internet to large readerships in most industrialized countries. For example, the puritanical, spiritually tinged 1989 book *Seven Habits of Highly Effective People* by U.S. business consultant Steven Covey has sold more than five million copies in over 40 countries.[22] Employing several hundred consultants, Covey has been offering management consulting and advice, and has provided retreats for managers including an introduction to so-called *wisdom literature*.[23] Throughout the 1990s writers and consulting firms providing prescriptive management models touching issues of *values* and *consciousness* in business and in workplace-organization, have tended to borrow rhetoric from religious revivalism and explicitly aiming at re-enchanting work and the workplace (Salamon 2000a & b). Generally, these discussions of spiritual values in work environments have also been concerned with increasing globalization. Central concepts debated in these texts — such as that of *spirituality* — are discussed as globally valid phenomena, addressed in holistic and monistic terms. Usually writers and speakers do not distin-

---

22. Thrift 1997, 43. Cefkin 1998, 112.
23. In a later expansion on this book, Stephen R. Covey writes: 'Character development is the best manifestation of our maturity. To value oneself and, at the same time, subordinate oneself to higher purposes and principles is the paradoxical essence of highest humanity and the foundation of effective leadership. Principle-centred leaders are men and women of character who work with competence "on farms" with "seed and soil" and who work in harmony with natural, "true north" principles and with the law of the harvest. They build those principles into the centre of their lives, into the centre of their relationships, into the centre of their communications and contracts, into their management processes, and into their mission statements'(1996), 1998, Covey Leadership Center and Franklin Covey, (http://www.franklincovey.com/ez/library).

guish between types of spiritual traditions, as they are convinced that all spiritual practices fundamentally stem from the same global source. I would like to discuss particular aspects of this *globalism* as it stands out as an ideal in certain spiritually-concerned management texts of the 1990s.

Philosophy of Business at a Global Level

The general globalistic ideal of the spiritually inspired management formation is well illustrated by the explicitly stated goals of consultant Richard Barrett, who wants 'to help organizations build cultural capital and release human potential' and is specialized in values-based *Corporate Transformation Tools®* and *Leadership Team Development Programs.*[24] Barrett sees it as his *mission* 'to change the philosophy of Business at a global level', and he wants to 'create a sustainable future for our children'. He assures that this is 'a win-win message for companies', thus guaranteeing that enterprise will not lose anything by applying his methods, whereas both sides in business interaction will come out as winners through the new approach. Barrett believes in 'making a difference by being different yourself' and his motto is 'Believing is seeing'. Educated as an engineer, he worked in the World Bank for several years, of which the last brought him to function as a *Values Co-ordinator* for the bank. Today he is a fellow of the World Business Academy, a group of business leaders and futurists meeting 'in various locales around the world' to work for 'a positive, sustainable society'. The sessions of the Academy 'were catalyzed by an awareness that a tidal wave of change was forecasted to wash over the international business community, and the entire globe, with unprecedented force'.[25]

'Going Global from the Inside Out'

The entire globe is also the concern of the founder of Consulting Network International, Inc. of New York, Cynthia F. Barnum. The title above is borrowed from her 1992 article 'Effective membership in the

24. Barrett 1998.
25. Statement by The World Business Academy, printed in Liebig 1994, 242.

global business community' printed in a non-academic style business management book entitled *New traditions in business. Spirit and leadership in the 21st century*. In the article Cynthia Barnum advocates an internalized *globalism*:

And because globalization requires a commitment that won't quit, it must become part of you, part of your belief and value system. To do this you have to personally *internalize* the global experience in a powerful way. Doing this will affect your most intimately held beliefs, but only you have the power to decide what's important at that core level. Unless globalization means something to this inner part of you, you will never become sufficiently motivated to acquire new attitudes, new skills, and the knowledge necessary to profit personally and professionally from globalization.[26]

Barnum then goes on to describe globalization as a 'paradigm shift'. She uses a language that could also have been employed to describe a religious conversion experience of perceived spiritual enlightenment:

Awareness of global interconnectedness is the key. Most globally aware individuals can tell you about the gradual process they experienced or the 'ah-ha' moment when they suddenly realized 'it's all one world'. From Earth Day to the Amazonian rainforest, it may have been their interest in ecology and the environment; for others it may have been actual travels, or exposure to international organizations like the United Nations or humanitarian relief agencies, even the Peace Corps. Space exploration has also contributed to the 'one world' realization [...] Whatever the source, being able to think and feel interconnected on a global level is what's causing the paradigm shift here. The world is borderless when seen from a high enough perspective, and this has all kinds of implications: socially, politically, economically, and even spiritually. [...] Regardless of how the awareness began, it generally culminates in a sense of global citizenship [...] The best approach is to develop a sense that 'I belong anywhere I am, no matter who I am' [...].[27]

26. Barnum 1992, 142 ff.
27. Ibid.

Barnum is preaching a globalism that clearly touches issues of cosmology and paradigmatic ontological teachings. Its self-promoting functionality — that one must adopt global awareness *in order* to profit personally and professionally — can be related to what Paul Heelas[28] has seen as New Age self-spirituality and self-actualization. Barnum's globally aware individual is self-spiritualized into believing in — or maybe rather accepting as a dogma — that the world is borderless and that the globalized individual who has accepted this truth belongs anywhere, any time, no matter the cultural and other contexts. The globalized individual has had her identity transformed, symbolized by a new 'virtual' citizenship (Barnum uses the metaphor of a 'global passport' 1992:146), allowing her to profit both personally and professionally. Barnum connects these virtues to the many advantages this will have for the business corporation to which the, by now, globally motivated individual belongs.

Cynthia Barnum's conjuring up of the new global existence is but one of a number of cultural manifestations in which old-style modernist universalism has been replaced by a post- or hyper-modernist individualistic globalism. Whereas modernist universalism implied generalized ambitions of creating equal conditions for humans, of making life conditions more similar or of creating a universal order of some kind, the post-modern globalism has no such ambitions. It is a-materialist, a-political and radically individualized.

Holism and Inner Development

The global must come from within each individual and can only arise from individual transformations of consciousness and values. In business organization and management strategy the old-style, bureaucratic, top-down, mechanistic systems of creating rational order in the production are viewed as negative, anti-human, mechanistic and void of spiritual enlightenment. Advocates of an organic, holistic, all-encompassing and spiritualized corporate culture criticize formerly established divisions between private and public, work and spare-time, the meaning of life for each worker and the goals of

28. Paul Heelas 1996.

the company for destroying harmony and wholeness in organizations. They perceive these divisions in social life as symptoms of a destructive 'fragmentation [that] pervades society — almost as a lifestyle, and can be found in each single organization and in each single individual. It leads to a confusion of our thinking, and this confusion creates an endless chain of problems [...]', as formulated by Danish professor of management studies, Steen Hildebrandt.[29] They also generally state that the overall goal of a company must be defined in relation to higher forces of life, and thus become part of a profound meaningfulness in life. The goal of the company can and should accordingly be encompassed in each individual worker's ideals of existence. The general life of employees must be in harmony with the *communitas*[30] of the corporation to which they belong.[31] The ideology is thus concerned with each organizational body *per se*, and in spite

29. Hildebrandt 1992, 9. My unauthorized translation from Danish.
30. Communitarian ideals seem to be generally accepted in the movement advocating love and spiritual approaches in the workplace. Juanita Brown, president of Whole Systems Associates, presents 'A Vision of Corporation as Community' in *Corporation As Community: A New Image for a New Era* (1992). She wants to develop the 'possibilities of designing organizations that can create a merger between the strengths of the corporation and the vitality of a healthy community' (op. cit. 127). Even if these types of visions do not exclude a universal adoption of their norms, they also do not explicitly work to include all of humankind, but focus on each workplace 'congregation' of employees as a communitarian island of its own (cf. Salamon 2000a & b).'I think the alternative to capitalism is not communism — it's community — and I think we are ready for that now' says Matthew Fox, ordained US Anglican priest (dismissed from the Dominican order in 1993 for his unorthodox positions), educator and the internationally known writer of more than 15 books that have sold over 700,000 copies in seven languages. Amongst his books is the title *The Reinvention of Work: A New Vision of Livelihood for Our Times* (Toms 1997, 73, 78).
31. Salamon 2000a quotes management researcher P. Pruzan for his discussion (in a lecture at Copenhagen Business School, 28 April 1998) of leadership in terms of integrity and authenticity as an 'agreement between private, personal values and the corporate values of management'. He finds that organizations lack integrity when the 'private values' of the manager are detached from those of the corporation.

of the universalist rhetoric of wholeness and globality, there seem to
be few ambitions of improving the totality of the world and bringing
enlightenment and prosperity to all of mankind. It is generally accepted that the inner development of individuals (self-development)
must preclude communal and societal progression. Evolution happens 'from the inside out'. In a conversation with Peter Russell, who
is an influential public speaker and author of *The Creative Manager.
Finding Inner Vision and Wisdom In Uncertain Times,*[32] I asked him if it
isn't so that the communal precludes 'inner development'. Russell replied 'I hope not! If so, Marx was right and I am wrong. The communal automatically follows from the inner development'.[33] Each
person must start with improving her/himself, each organization
must transform itself, and then maybe change will happen on a larger
scale.

Borderless is Rising

Whereas the sun never set in Queen Victoria's world empire, it was
not globalistic in the sense of the writers I quote here. It was imperial
and aimed to eradicate all un-colonized, white spots on the map.
Also, even if today the sun never sets on the transnational financial
system, the cosmology is different. It implies a view of society as a
hybrid, morphing form in which multitudes of individual cells communicate and exchange, but in which no higher order is either existing or wished. The metaphorical white spots on the map do not at-
tract much interest, as there is no articulated focus on including all of
mankind in the project. Rather, the global situation presents opportunities for the individual to gain self-knowledge, greater consciousness of existence and greater opportunities for living out dreams and
potentials.[34] Globality is a condition of removed obstacles, not of any

32. Russell & Evans 1992.
33. From my fieldwork notes, *The 1998 International Conference on Business and
    Consciousness*, Mexico.
34. During fieldwork (1998) in a Californian arranged conference, situated on
    the Mexican Pacific coast, I had a talk with two of the trend-setters, con-
    sultants and advocates of wisdom-based management. One of them is a
    Los Angeles radio host, therapist and writer, the other is a London based
    international management-writer and speaker. The latter told the radio

particular world order. Advertisements of recent years are examples of this, and well in line with the writers presented above. United Airlines had an advertisement in *Wired* magazine saying:

Travel, by definition, suggests you move. We are doing what we can to remove obstacles. We can't change the weather. But we can empower our employees to resolve problems when they arise. [...] Borderless is rising. A single check-in at your first gate. Passage to anywhere your mind has ever wandered. We're getting close [...] we're forming partnerships both regionally and globally with other airlines to co-ordinate and expedite your passage. It's the way the world looks from the air, not from the map. United is rising.[35]

Clearly, the global condition ideally portrayed here is only for the few — for those elites who have earned their right to belong to those for whom obstacles are removed. Another globalistic advertisement formulates it this way:

Now that you have a global agenda, it's time you had a global phone. [...] It allows you to speak to anyone, virtually anywhere on the planet. To stay connected with a single, worldwide telephone number. And to communicate where others cannot. Iridium is here. Call now and send a message to the world. Iridium. Calling planet Earth.[36]

host that he had some bad days at the moment 'when I can't really see the mission — the purpose in what I do'. But he then concluded that it was probably just a 'mid-writing phase' because of his new book. He intended to go to LA right after the conference (in November), then on to England in December-January, then to Australia and New Zealand in February and then maybe on to an island off the coast of Mexico, where he had a friend, who has had 'a place' for 30 years, and where you can only go by boat. 'But that is probably just another of my dreams...' It is too cumbersome to move geographically. 'It takes me a few days to get used to new places. And then I don't have my notes for the book with me...'. This conversation is typical for the globetrotting consultancy elites, who are some of the main articulators of the discourse of globalism.
35. *Wired Magazine*, March and May issues, 1999.
36. *Wired Magazine*, May 1999.

It is significant here that the privileged globalized individual here can communicate *where others cannot*. He can move where others cannot — all within a single network. The world is *one place* for him and he has a message to the world. He is constructed as a privileged, communicating prophet of global consciousness. Here a single individual (or a single corporate body of *communitas*[37]) contains the global. The global is not a complete and universal totality containing lots of these liberated and solidarized individuals. The globalistic individual here is achieving his global, privileged identity through the very contrast existing between his life-conditions and those of the popular masses of the Earth, who are contained within the obstacles of their non-globalized condition. Sociologist Zygmunt Bauman writes about the 'new weightlessness of power'. He describes a power constituted through the ability to move and move away *from*.[38] To be non-territorial, have weightless capital, free from any bonds of responsibility towards a local community. In the new global system, the privileged possess deterritorialized power. The others — the majority of the world's population — are evermore under surveillance and territorialized, contained by the similarly territorialized ground-forces such as the police, the armies and the micro-panoptical surveillance of computer communications in supermarkets and troubled-neighbourhoods. Getting access to new territory and crossing borders and boundaries are privileges that are under close surveillance and heavily controlled and are objects of very heated political and popular-cultural debates these years. Being globalized implies that one is lifted above such everyday, trivial battles. Communications- and cultural studies researcher Lawrence Grossberg finds that 'globalization is the ideology of contemporary capitalism through which capitalism attempts to naturalize and legitimate itself and thus disable resistance'.[39]

Mono-Cultural Celebrations of Diversity

On the other side of the table, so to say, the management-consultants P. Prasad and A.J. Mills worry '[...] that workplace diversity and multiculturalism may well be in danger of becoming trendy consumer

37. See Salamon 2000a.
38. Bauman 1998.
39. Grossberg 1999, 14.

items marketed in the form of executive seminars, t-shirts and mugs, museum exhibits and workplace training schedules'.[40] The two authors thus see a tendency towards a *commodification of diversity* taking place in the North American culture where they primarily work. It is a culture, they write, where any revolutionary idea or reform movement is turned into a popular entertainment item or fashionable piece of memorabilia. They are concerned that serious movements during this process become turned into short-lived fleeting (we may add — politically harmless) fads. In the management texts and management training seminars I have studied, I have noticed a similar *commodification* of multiculturalism and also of various spiritual reform movements in the business world. The *glob*al is celebrated in a number of cultural festivals, pick-and-choose use of traditional rituality and so forth, but the mono-culturalism of the work practises and the all-encompassing capitalist consumer culture remain relatively unchanged. When I did fieldwork at the *1998 International Conference on Business and Consciousness* in Puerto Vallarta in Mexico, hundreds of business consultants and executives from around 20 nations went through rituals such as the so-called *Dances of Universal Peace*,[41] honouring all spiritual world-traditions, as it was said. The event included chant for Krishna, recitation of Sufi love mysticism, medieval Spanish, Christian Aramaic and biblical Hebrew songs that all were

---

40. Prasad and Mills 1997, 14
41. In the words of those actively involved in the movement, 'The *Dances of Universal Peace* are joyous and meditative circle dances which honor the spiritual traditions of the world. They integrate simple folk dance movements with songs and chants from many of the world's sacred traditions [...] Participants dance together without performers or audience, creating an easily accessible celebration of unity' (http://meditation.hnt.com/dup.html).
   These dances 'help create peace and unity. The *Dances of Universal Peace* were originated by the American mystic Samuel Lewis (1896-1971) as part of his vision of "Peace through the Arts." Some of the traditions represented are American Indian, Jewish, Hindu, Buddhist, Sufi, Christian, Zoroastrian, Islamic, Goddess, Celtic and Universalist. The Dances are easy and fun to do. No experience is necessary, all are welcome. We don't use any electronic form of music' (http://www.atri.curtin.edu.au/~tonys/bio/dup_short.html).

supposed to sing together whilst dancing in a circle with the other men and women present. The organizers told me that they felt ecumenically global and in respect of cultural hybridity. They did not share my experience of facing a holistic, monistic, markedly Western and mainly Christian rooted discourse of universalism and globalism. To the organizers of the business conference and most of my fellow-participants in the dance, the *Universal* dances represented the cosmological and spiritual approach they want to introduce in corporate settings.

Global Encompasses *all*

In a talk with manager and writer James E. Liebig, process consultant of Minneapolis, Barbara Shipka, observes that though the word *global* may often be used in a jargon sense in business, it implies greater inclusivity than the word *international*. Global encompasses *all*. Furthermore, she notes, the word implies more than physical geography. She views the physical poverty she has witnessed in Africa, Asia, and South America as being analogous to the spiritual poverty she sees in corporate settings:

The same way that food is nourishment for people who are starving physically, authenticity is nourishment for people who are starving spiritually. The way the workplace is set up, it can starve us spiritually [...] In our culture we have attached our identity to our careers, and if the job is a place where you live in fear, that's an impoverished life. [42]

Speaking of the consultant work, Shipka adds:

[...] when I haven't had enough business, I thought maybe I should define things more. Yet when I let go, the divinity of what I'm doing, the support of the divine, comes right in. So not getting too contained around the business is related to the fact that this is a partnership with a larger system. [43]

42. Liebig 1994, 180-81.
43. Liebig 1994, 182.

Shipka's statements illustrate the merging of private and work spheres, a globalist cosmology viewing existence as holistic and monistic, and the application of neo-spiritual beliefs in the workplace. As in the Universal Dances at the business conference, Shipka's global perspective has a somewhat spiritual quality and it encompasses all. The physical poverty of the territorially bound and unprivileged masses is analogized with the spiritual poverty of the corporate employees — who are also often the deterritorialized elites of the privileged world. Shipka's solution to spiritual poverty is defined as authenticity. Authenticity is related to acknowledging a holistic and monistic reality, and to letting the support of the divine come into the workplace. Thus, the global is not a matter of geography, nor is it purely a matter of trade-relations. The way the term global is being used in texts on new spiritual traditions in business — such as that of Shipka talking with Liebig — also implies a monistic and holistic world-system. As I see it, Globalism is thus a (post-) modern cosmology of a privileged, deterritorialising consumer culture. In this context private and public, spiritual conviction and material consumption, tourism and mission, family-life and work merge. Accordingly, Barbara Shipka exemplifies her own ideology by dissolving any distinction between private life and business:

A new level in her search for her own authenticity and passion for global community began recently when she went to Peru and adopted an Amazon Indian infant. She is excited to watch a new life unfolded in him. 'At the micro-level, I'm actually seeing a soul manifest itself on Earth! And I'm also discovering that by bringing that human part of me into business, I have been able to allow other people to be more human. If Michael is sick, I get to learn about my clients' families, too.[44]

Aiming for the Perfectly Global

The kind of values voiced in these few examples I have given here of texts and other voices concerned with values and spirituality in busi-

44. Op. cit. 183.

ness, are influential today in the organising of corporate workforces. This is particularly the case in North America and Europe, but also elsewhere in the English-speaking world, in Latin America, and to a lesser extent in Asia. It is a field of cultural expression where market-ideology and private spiritual convictions merge. The combination can be understood as a result of a work-market and production system, where the most qualified knowledge-workers are too few to fill all job positions in the corporate landscape, and a need for finding other work incentives than higher salaries has arisen in corporations. It can also be understood in the context of the very real politics of the deterritorialising of power structures taking place during the process of economic and demographic globalization.[45] I believe that the new globalism as a cosmology — maybe of a fleeting kind — must be understood in this context. Management training and consultancies is an area of socio-cultural practice, where this combination of altered power structures and alternative cosmology has become conspicuous. The training of corporate workforces to become believers in *globalism* — the globalization of the New Age — has very real consequences for the functioning of transnational corporations, for the leaders of our present economy and thus for the world system.

Today, the global is taken to be a fact of life, and globalism an ideal cosmology to suit this. At least in the versions I have presented here, it is a cosmology of a New Age type. It is 'self-religious' and whilst sometimes voicing Universalist ideals, it is not practically interested in modernist universal programmes of large-scale, organized order-creation and human equality. It is concerned with the individual living in a corporate community. It tends to *commodify* identity into what I want to call *instant identity*; a non-obliging access to short-term, but highly intensive communitas, that can be cast away and replaced with the next move of career. As I see it, this corporate globalism is a symbolic language and a strong cultural discourse of being (or aiming to become) part of the deterritorialized elites, to whom time and

---

45. As mentioned in the first part of this article, it can still be debated to what extent our present world-economy is more or less 'global' than earlier, e.g. colonial economies.

space are no longer obstacles to the acquisition of all that is left to be conquered. Time and space 'are now to be transcended in the imaginary of the perfectly global'.[46] I find this globalism to be part of a contemporary trend that re-articulates business and the corporate world into something meaningfully spiritual and cultural — into a matter of existential values for the individual employee (and customer). It thus individualizes ritual experience and celebrates experiences of an 'authenticity' that it also simultaneously constructs as a perennialist[47] mythology of holistic monism, neglecting materialist analytical understandings and historical perspectives. It attempts to reconstruct the workplace as a holistic community of positive believers and business as a spiritual pursuit, all within the Oneness of global capitalism.

Bibliography

Barnet, Richard J. and John Cavanagh 1995. *Global Dreams. Imperial Corporations and the New World Order.* New York: Touchstone, Simon & Schuster.

Barnum, Cynthia F. 1992. 'Effective Membership in the Global Business Community'. In: John Renesch (ed.), *New Traditions in Business. Spirit and Leadership in the 21st Century.* San Francisco: Berrett-Koehler.

Barrett, Richard, et al. 1998. 'Cultural Transformation and Leadership Development Consultants'. *Supporting Leaders in Building Values-Driven Organizations.* (http://www.corptools.com/index.shtml)

---

46. Smith 1997, 11.
47. '[...] New Agers are perennialists. [...] Unity firmly prevails over diversity. Having little or no faith in the external realm of traditional belief, New Agers can ignore apparently significant differences between religious traditions [...] But they do have faith in that wisdom which is experienced as lying at the heart of the religious domain as a whole. From the de-traditionalized stance of the New Age what matters is the [...] 'ageless wisdom'. And, it can be added, New Agers attach equal importance — because it is an aspect of the spiritual realm as a whole — to the essential unity of the human species, scorning nationally or ethnically differentiated modes of being' (Heelas 1996, 27).

Bauman, Zygmunt 1998. *Globalization — The human consequences.* Cambridge: Polity Press.

Bicheno, John 2000. *The Lean Toolbox.* Second Edition. Buckingham, England: PICSIE Books.

Brown, Juanita 1992. 'Corporation As Community: A New Image for a New Era'. In: John Renesch (ed.), *New Traditions in Business. Spirit and Leadership in the 21st Century.* San Francisco: Berrett-Koehler.

Brown, Tom 1999. 'Intuition Really Is Hidden Intelligence'. *Management General,* website newsletter. (http://www.mgeneral.com/1-lines/99-lines/051999li.htm).

Cefkin, Melissa 1998. 'Toward a Higher-Order Merger. A Middle-Manager's Story'. In: George E. Marcus (Ed.), *Corporate Futures. The Diffusion of the Culturally Sensitive Corporate Form.* Chicago: University of Chicago Press, Late Editions.

Covey, Stephen R. 1992. *The Seven Habits of Highly Effective People. Powerful Lessons in Personal Change.* London: Simon & Schuster.

Dahle, Cheryl 1999. 'What's Your Intuition about Consultants? We have a feeling they're full of it — intuition, that is. *Fast Company* 15, 50.

Drucker, Peter 1977. *Management.* An abridged and revised version of *Management: Tasks, Responsibilities, Practices.* London: Pan Books (in association with Heinemann).

Friedman, Jonathan 1990. 'Being in the World: Globalization and Localization'. In: Mike Featherstone (ed.), *Global Culture. Nationalism, Globalization and Modernity.* London: Sage.

Giddens, Anthony 1991. *Modernity and Self-Identity. Self and Society in the Late Modern Age.* Calif.: Stanford University Press.

Grossberg, Lawrence 1999. 'Speculations and Articulations of Globalization', *Polygraph* 11, 11-48.

Harrington, Anne 1996. *Reenchanted Science. Holism in German Culture from Wilhelm II to Hitler.* New Jersey: Princeton University Press.

Heelas, Paul 1996. *The New Age Movement.* Oxford: Blackwell.

Hildebrandt, Steen 1992. 'Fragmentering contra helhedssyn — På vej mod helhedssyn i ledelsespraksis'. In: Steen Hildebrandt and Leif H. Alken (eds.), *På vej mod helhedssyn i ledelse... billeder fra praksis.* Hinnerup: Forlaget Ankerhus.

Hirst, Paul 1997. *Globalisering, demokrati og det civile samfund.* Copenhagen: Hans Reitzels Forlag.

Ingold, Tim 1993. 'Globes and Spheres: the Topology of Environmentalism'. In: Kay Milton (ed.), *Environmentalism. The View from Anthropology.* (*ASA Monograph* 32). London: Routledge.

Kunde, Jesper 1997. *Corporate Religion. Vejen til en stærk virksomhed.* Copenhagen: Børsen.

Liebig, James E. 1994. *Merchants of Vision. People Bringing New Purpose and Values to Business.* San Francisco: Berrett-Koehler (in cooperation with The World Business Academy).

Low, Albert 1993. *Zen and Creative Management.* Boston: Charles E. Tuttle.

Luhmann, Niklas 1997. 'Globalization or World Society: How to Conceive of Modern Society?' *International Review of Sociology,* 7/1.

Prasad, Pushkala and Albert J. Mills 1997. 'From Showcase to Shadow: Understanding the Dilemmas of Managing Workplace Diversity'. In: P. Prasad, A. Mills and Michael Elmes (eds.), *Managing the Organizational Melting Pot: Dilemmas of Workplace Diversity,* Thousand Oaks, Calif.: Sage.

Russell, Peter and Roger Evans 1992. *The Creative Manager. Finding Inner Vision and Wisdom In Uncertain Times.* San Francisco: Jossey-Bass Inc.

Rutte, Martin 1998. 'Spirituality in the Workplace'. (Updated version of an article that first appeared in the business book *Heart at Work* by Jack Canfield and Jacqueline Miller). New York: McGraw-Hill.

Rutte, Martin 1998. *Spirituality in the workplace.* Hosted by Martin Rutte, http://www.martinrutte.com/welcome.html.

Sadler, William 1994. *The I Ching of Management. An Age-Old Study for New Age Managers.* Atlanta, Georgia: Humanics Publishing Group.

Salamon, Karen Lisa G. 2000a. 'No Borders in Business: The management discourse of organisational holism'. In: Timothy Bewes and Jeremy Gilbert (eds), *Cultural Capitalism. Politics after New Labour* London: Lawrence & Wishart, 134-57.

Salamon, Karen Lisa G. 2000b. 'Faith Brought to Work: A spiritual movement in business management'. *Anthropology in Action. Journal for Applied Anthropology in Policy and Practice,* 7/3.

Senge, Peter M. 1992. 'The Leader's New Work: Building Learning Organizations'. In: John Renesch (ed.), *New Traditions in Business. Spirit and Leadership in the 21st Century*. San Francisco: Berrett-Koehler.

Smith, Paul 1997. *Millennial Dreams. Contemporary Culture and Capital in the North*. London: Verso.

Thrift, Nigel 1997. 'The Rise of Soft Capitalism'. *Cultural Values* Vol.1(1), 29-57.

Toms, Michael 1997. *The Soul of Business*. Carlsbad, Calif.: Hay House Inc. (in cooperation with New Dimensions).

Wired Magazine, March and May issues, 1999.

Wolf, Eric 1982. *Europe and the People without History*. Berkeley: University of California Press.

Contributors

Liselotte Frisk
Lecturer, PhD, Högskolan Dalarna, Department of Religion.
Address: 791 88 Falun, Sweden.

Ingvild Sælid Gilhus
Professor, Dr.phil., Department of the History of Religions, University of Bergen.
Address: Öisteinsgate 3, N-5007, Bergen, Norway.

Wouter J. Hanegraaff
Professor, Dr., Department of Theology & Religious Studies, University of Amsterdam.
Address: Faculty of Humanities, Oude Turfmarkt 147, NL-1012 GC Amsterdam, The Netherlands.

Olav Hammer
Associate professor, PhD, Department of Theology & Religious Studies, University of Amsterdam.
Address: Faculty of Humanities, Oude Turfmarkt 147, NL-1012 GC Amsterdam, The Netherlands.

Massimo Introvigne
Dr., Director, Center for the Study of New Religions (CESNUR).
Address: Via Confienza 19, 10121 Torino, Italy.

J. Gordon Melton
Director, Institute for the Study of American Religions (ISAR).
Address: P.O. Box 90709, Santa Barbara, Calif. 93190-0709, USA.

Lisbeth Mikaelsson
Associate professor, Dr. phil. Department of the History of Religions, University of Bergen.
Address: Öisteinsgate 3, N-5007, Bergen, Norway.

Mikael Rothstein
Associate Professor, MA & PhD., Department of History of Religions, University of Copenhagen.
Address: Artillerivej 86, DK-2300 Copenhagen S, Denmark.

Karen Lisa Goldschmidt Salamon
Research Fellow, MSc, Department of Management, Politics and Philosophy, Copenhagen Business School.
Address: Blaagaardsgade 23B, DK-2200 Copenhagen N, Denmark.

Index of Persons